The World in a Nutshell

China

in a nutshell

*

Enisen Publishing

China in a Nutshell

*China's flag, first flown the day the PRC was founded, October 1, 1949, is composed of a red background with five gold stars in the upper left corner. The color scheme is similar to that of the flag of the former Soviet Union, with red symbolizing the blood of martyrs who died in the cause of revolution, and gold representing a bright and golden future. By most accounts, the large star symbolizes the leadership of the Communist party. The other four represent either the Four Occupations, an ancient hierarchical class comprising the gentry, artisans and craftsmen, peasant farmers and merchants or the four, most esteemed occupations according to the Communist Party of China: farmers, workers, teachers and soldiers. Other interpretations claim the five stars represent the Communist Party and four subordinate parties or China's five ethnic groups (Han, Manchus, Mongols, Hui or Uighurs and Tibetans – although this interpretation could have been confused with the five-colored-stripe flag design briefly adopted by the Republic of China (1912-1928). Between 1928 and 1929, the Chinese flew the National Flag of the Republic of China (a canton of twelve white sun rays in a blue sky within a "red earth" background). The flag was controversially adopted in Taiwan after the defeat of the Nationalists by the Communists in 1949.

Qing Flag (1890-1912)   ROC Flag (1912-1928)   ROC Flag (1928-1949)

Note: This book uses the initials B.C. ("before Christ") and A.D. ("Anno Domini" or "in the year of our Lord") rather than B.C.E. ("Before the Common Era") and C.E. (in the Common Era") to designate time periods since the writer and editors felt these terms were more familiar to Nutshell Notes readers.

We understand that future activities may modify or shed new light on some of the data in this book. For that reason, Nutshell Notes, LLC and Enisen Publishing invite readers to visit our websites www.enisen.com and www.worldinanutshell.com to learn about the latest developments concerning China.

China in a Nutshell
First published – June 2009
First edition – June 2009

Enisen Publishing
2118 Wilshire Boulevard, #351
Santa Monica, CA 90403-5784
http://www.enisen.com
publishing@enisen.com

Text	Amanda Roraback
Maps	Katie Gerber
Editor-in-Chief	D.A. Roraback

A special thank you to M.R. without whose help this book could not have been completed.

ISBN: 978-0-9763070-2-0

Printed in the United States of America

TABLE OF CONTENTS

Maps

Boxes and Sidebars

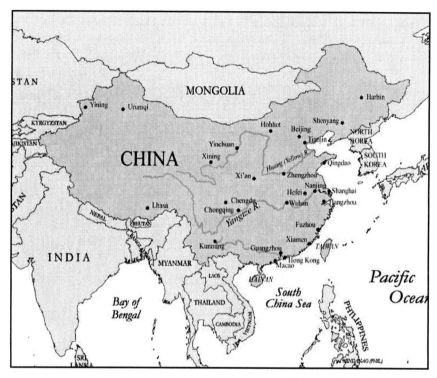

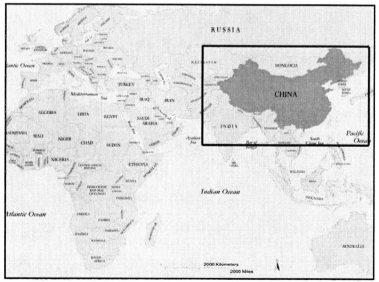

FACTS AND FIGURES

Name: People's Republic of China (PRC)

Local: Long form: Zhonghua Renmin Gongheguo

Geography: 9,596,960 sq km, slightly smaller than the United States. World's fourth largest country (after Russia, Canada, U.S.). Mount Everest, on China's border with Nepal, is the world's highest peak.

Capital City: Beijing. Largest city: Shanghai

Exex. Branch: President Hu Jintao, Vice President Xi Jinping, Premier Wen Jiabao, Exec. Vice Premier Li Keqiang, Vice Premiers Hui Liangyu, Zhang Deijiang and Wang Qishan.

Admin. Div.: 23 provinces (incl. Taiwan), 5 autonomous regions (incl. Xizang [Tibet]), 4 municipalities (incl. Beijing and Shanghai) and 2 special administrative regions (Hong Kong and Macau).

Independence: October 1, 1949 (People's Republic of China established)

Population: 1,338,612,968 (July 2009 est.) Pop. Growth: 0.655% (2009)

Life expect.: 73.47 years

Ethnic Groups:Han Chinese 91.5%, Zhuang, Hui, Uighur, Yi, Miao, Manchu, Tibetan, Mongol, Buyi (Bouyei), Tujia, Korean, and others 8.5%

Religions: (China is officially atheist) Daoist (Taoist), Buddhist, Christian 3%-4%, Muslim 1%-2%

Languages: Mandarin (Putonghua), Yue (Cantonese), Wu (Shanghainese), Minbei (Fuzhou), Minnan (Hokkien-Taiwanese), Xiang, Gan, Hakka dialects, minority languages

Literacy: Total population: 90.9%

Currency: *Renminbi* (also referred to as the *yuan*)

Military: Peoples Liberation Army (PLA), 2.3 million active troops (world's largest standing army)

Oil product.: 3.73 million bbl/day, Oil Consumption: 6.93 million bbl/day

Export partners: U.S. 21%, Hong Kong 16%, Japan 9.5%, South Korea 4.6%, Germany 4.2%

Import partners: Japan 14.6%, South Korea 11.3%, Taiwan 10.9%, U.S. 7.5%, Germany 4.8%

GDP per capita: $6,100 (2008 est.) (tens of millions of people living in rural areas earn less than $125 a year).

Envir. issues: Air pollution (from reliance on coal); water shortages, esp. in the north; water pollution from untreated wastes; deforestation; estimated loss of 1/5th of agricultural land since 1949 to soil erosion and economic development; desertification; trade in endangered species

Figures taken from the CIA World Factbook 2009 – China

ANCIENT HISTORY

LEGEND OF PANGU

According to a Chinese legend, the universe was once a dark, mass of chaos until, many thousands of years ago, the cosmos began to form into an egg. Growing within this egg was a giant named **Pangu**, who emerged one day to create the world. For the next 18,000 years, Pangu put himself between the earth and the heavens and slowly separated the two. Once the sky and the earth were 30,000 miles apart, Pangu died and his remains transformed into the world's elements. Pangu's breath became the wind and the clouds, his voice became thunder, his eyes the sun and the moon, his blood the rivers, his hair became grass and finally, the fleas from his fur became human beings.

XIA DYNASTY (21st century – 16th century B.C.)

Of a slightly less mythological nature (but still doubted by many historians), the Chinese believe that China was first unified by **Yu the Great** (or **Dayu**), an ancient hero who tamed the torrential floods that had wreaked havoc for centuries, by digging canals that followed the natural courses of the **Yellow River**[1] or **Huang** (yellow) **He** (river) and planting trees along the banks.

When Yu died, the ministers passed the throne to his son, marking the first time rule was passed to a family member rather than the most capable leader, thereby introducing China's first hereditary dynasty.

Sixteen leaders are said to have succeeded Yu in the course of more than 400 years. The last ruler was purportedly a corrupt, tyrannical emperor who was overthrown by the leader of the Shang tribe from the east.

SHANG DYNASTY (16th century – 12th century B.C.)

Much evidence of the Shang Dynasty has been excavated from royal tombs near Anyang in the Henan Province in the form of bronze, jade and oracle bones. During this period, questions were inscribed on tortoise shells or bones that were heated causing them to crack.[2] The answers were determined by the shape of the cracks as interpreted by diviners (or priests). The inscriptions offered historians a trove of information about harvests, weather patterns, the activities of the emperor and religious and supernatural beliefs among other things. The Shang believed in a number of nature deities and a supreme god (**Shangdi**), the reputed ancestor of the Shang, who reigned in heaven and controlled the elements.

---

[1] The Yellow River, the 2nd largest river in China (after the Yangtze) and the 6th largest in the world is considered the birthplace of Chinese civilization and China's "mother river" because it has provided irrigation and drinking water for much of the Chinese population. Millions of people have drowned in the river's devastating floods. Today, the Chinese are more concerned with the Yellow River's shrinking water flow and resulting water shortages due to huge increases in water consumption by industrial and agricultural sectors along the river's valley.

[2] The Shang people made all important decisions based on the outcome of the oracle bones.

The favor of Shangdi and other deities could be acquired through various rituals and sacrifices and by appeasing the souls of one's ancestors. Some of these rituals were conducted using ornate vessels made of bronze – attesting to the Shang civilization's mastery of metallurgy. Also found in excavated tombs were the remains of horse-drawn carriages and sophisticated ceramics.

The Shang dynasty lasted for hundreds of years until the last emperor was overthrown by a chief of the Zhou tribe from the west.

ZHOU DYNASTY (1122 – 221 B.C.)

The Zhou legitimized the overthrow of the Shang and the rise of the Zhou by claiming that the Shang emperors had lost the mandate (authority) bestowed on them by heaven (*Shangdi*) because they had become corrupt and incapable rulers. The **Mandate of Heaven**, it was acknowledged, could only be sustained by a leader who maintained harmony between heaven and earth, acted ethically, and promoted the welfare of the people.

The early Zhou leaders, including **King Wen** (who first inherited the Mandate of Heaven) and his sons, King Wu and the Duke of Zhou,[3] lived in their capital in the western part of the empire (in present-day Xi'an) where they essentially adopted Shang rituals, administration techniques, writing systems and lifestyle (the **"Western Zhou"** period). In 771, attacks by barbarians and the death of the 37th emperor (**Yu Wang**) forced the Zhou to relocate to the east, beginning the **Eastern Zhou** period (770-221 B.C.).

DYNASTIES AT A GLANCE	
Xia Dynasty	c. 21st c.– 16th c.B.C.
Shang Dynasty	c. 16th c.– 12th c.B.C.
Zhou Dynasty	c. 1122-221 B.C.
Qin Dynasty	221-206 B.C.
Han Dynasty	206 B.C.– A.D. 220
3 Kingdoms Period	220 – 280
Jin Dynasty	265-420
N. & S. Dynasties	420-581
Sui Dynasty	581-618
Tang Dynasty	618-907
5 Dynasties/ 10 States	907-960
Song Dynasty	960-1279
Yuan Dynasty	1279-1368
Ming Dynasty	1368-1644
Qing Dynasty	1644-1911

Note: Dynasty dates may differ slightly in other historical sources.

The Zhou rulers governed the vast empire by dividing it into dozens of provinces

---

[3] The Chinese philosopher, Confucius (551-479 B.C.), regarded the era of King Wen, King Wu and the Duke of Zhou as a "golden age."

and endowing feudal lords (or vassals) with the power to rule over smaller regions in exchange for their loyalty. In time, the central government became weaker and some of the lords grew wealthier and more powerful by battling others for territory and hegemony. More than 450 battles waged by warlords tarnished the first three hundred years of the Eastern Zhou Dynasty (named the "**Spring and Autumn Period**" in the earliest Chinese historical text compiled by Confucius). The succeeding years (from the mid 5th century B.C. to 221 B.C., called the **Warring States Period**) were even more turbulent eventually resulting in the emergence of seven major states (Han, Zhao, Wei, Yan, Chu, Qi and Qin) that competed for complete control.

The upheaval, instability and immorality of the Eastern Zhou period drove intellectuals to formulate remedies to cure the deficiencies in the government and society. This intellectual fervor ushered in one of the most culturally rich and significant periods in Chinese history. Among the many philosophical creeds that made up the **Hundred Schools of Thought** were **Confucianism**, **Daoism** and **Legalism**. (See pgs. 73-74)

Confucianism, founded by **Kong Fuzi** or **Confucius**, posited that harmony could only transpire under the rule of benevolent and virtuous leaders.

Daoism (or **Taoism**), traditionally attributed to the semi-legendary philosopher **Laozi**, celebrated the perfect harmony that existed in nature and promoted man's withdrawal from the artificial structure of the world in pursuit of the "way" (or *dao*) – the force behind the natural order of the universe.

The followers of **Legalism** believed that human beings were essentially evil and needed to be governed by strict, punitive laws.

QIN[4] DYNASTY (221-206 B.C.)
In 221 B.C. the **Qin**, the most militarily advanced (though not necessarily culturally advanced) of the seven states under the Zhou defeated the others and unified the country.

The Qin's first emperor, **Qin Shi Huang Di**, who ascended the throne at age 13, ruled harshly and absolutely according to the tenets of Legalism which was adopted as the state's philosophy. Qin Shi Huang Di abolished the vassal system and stripped the nobles of their power.

In order to unify the country under his rule, the emperor standardized the currency (since the 6th century B.C., bronze spade-shaped money was used in central

---

[4] Also called the Chin Dynasty where the name "China" likely originated.

China and knife-shaped coins were used in the north and east), made weights and measures uniform throughout the country and designated a standard width between chariot wheels so that the wheels would fall in the same ruts on the roads. He standardized the written language – which had varied greatly from region to region during the Warring States period. He also attempted to abolish all divergent views by destroying documents that advocated different forms of government (along with the archives of defeated states),[5] and buried alive hundreds of scholars who opposed his rule. Rival armies were all disbanded and privately owned weapons were seized to prevent any possibility of revolt.

Qin Shi Huang Di also forced peasants to work as laborers on massive construction projects including highways, canals and irrigation works as well as a huge wall with watchtowers built at intervals (the forerunner of the modern **Great Wall** [6]), that connected a number of defensive barriers to protect the country from invasion by the barbarian **Huns (Xiongnu)** to the north of the empire.

Qin Shi Huang Di was forever seeking a magical elixir for immortality. In case the potions didn't work, he also planned for a regal life after death by ordering hundreds of thousands of workmen to design and build a huge "army" of life-sized terracotta clay soldiers [7] to be placed in a giant tomb that would be filled with precious objects. To protect the tomb from intruders, the workers poured in rivers of poisonous liquid mercury and installed automatic crossbows that would be triggered by any disturbance.

Wearied by the endless public works and high taxes imposed to pay for the grandiose projects, the peasants revolted within months after Qin's death. They were joined by soldiers and the nobility who were bitter because of the loss of their power. Qin Shi Huang Di's weak successor was powerless against the mobs and submitted to **Liu Bang** (later known as **Emperor Gao**), a peasant who rose from the ranks to become a minor commander in the Qin army, and who declared himself emperor of the **Han Dynasty** in 206 B.C.

The Qin dynasty was short-lived but left a lasting legacy. Qin

---

[5] Among the destroyed history books were those written by Confucius that glorified the Zhou Dynasty. Details of Qin Shi Huang Di's life were recorded in Sima Qian's <u>Records of the Grand Historian</u> – the definitive source of Chinese history up to the Han Dynasty.

[6] There is little remaining of Qin Shi Huang Di's wall. The Great Wall visible today was primarily built in the 16th century during the Ming Dynasty.

[7] Excavations of the tombs in Xi'an revealing the life-sized clay soldiers began in 1974 and can be visited today.

Shi Huang Di's tyrannical application of Legalism was largely reversed in the early Han dynasty but elements of the Legalist system remained: centralized bureaucratic government; collective responsibility for the actions of individuals and the assumption of guilt in criminal cases, for example, remained part of mainstream Chinese law.

HAN DYNASTY (206 B.C. to A.D. 220)

The Han Dynasty period was considered so glorious that the vast majority of Chinese today still refer to themselves as ethnically Han, the largest single ethnic group in the world.[8] The empire at this time even rivaled the Roman Empire in size, population and influence.

Unlike their reviled predecessors who imposed brutal punishments to keep the people in line, the Han rulers adopted Confucian ideals believing that governance was more effective if guided by a code of morality and integrity. Although centralized government was maintained, several feudal states were developed. In order to prevent the nobles from taking over, the Han government for the first time selected advisors on the basis of skill, ability and the knowledge of Confucian classics rather than lineage or wealth. The new system, in theory, gave serfs and commoners the opportunity to enter the service of the court.[9]

With capable administrators in the government, the empire made great strides economically and militarily – especially during the reign of **Emperor Wu** (140-87 B.C.), dubbed the "Martial Emperor." In the 2nd century B.C., China's borders expanded into northern Vietnam, Korea, Manchuria and north of the Gobi desert in Hun territory. The non-Chinese states were allowed to maintain their autonomy as long as they accepted the Han as their overlords.

The relative peace on China's borders greatly stimulated the exchange of goods and ideas between Asia and Europe by making passage safe along the **Silk Road**, a 5,000 mile series of trade roots traversing an area between

---

[8] Over 90% of the population of China (about 1.2 billion) consider themselves descendants of the Han Dynasty.

[9] Until the 20th century, government appointments and bureaucratic advancement were determined by scores received on standardized Civil Service exams open to all people. But although peasants and the poor were permitted to sit the exams, most could not afford tutors or take time away from their work to prepare for the tests.

China and the Mediterranean Sea from present-day Xi'an to Asia Minor. The opening of the Silk Road (named after China's most profitable trade commodity, silk[10]) brought foreign goods to China (for example, horses from Iran and musical instruments from Central Asia) and exposed the Chinese to foreign cultures, in particular **Buddhism**. In turn, the Chinese introduced the Romans to the crossbow, silk and other Chinese goods.

By A.D. 9, the Han Empire had stretched beyond the ability of the Emperor to govern and corruption and mismanagement plagued the ruling house. For the next 15 years, consequently, the empire was governed by **Wang Mang**, a reformer from the landholding class who had seized the throne in A.D. 9 and embarked on a series of radical reforms. He was overthrown by a secret society of peasants known as the **Red Eyebrows** (because they painted their eyebrows red) in collaboration with members of the royal Han family thereby restoring the dynasty.

Under the **Eastern Han** or "Later" Han (A.D. 25-220), as the dynasty was now called, Chinese industry greatly improved and a number of inventions came into being, most significantly the invention of **paper**[11] at the beginning of the 2nd century A.D., which made the creation of books cheaper and facilitated the spread of literacy and knowledge. (The process did not reach the Middle East until the 6th century and it was not until 1151 that the first paper mill was built in Europe.)

The Han began to disintegrate again in the second century as the court degenerated under the rule of younger and more incompetent rulers who were attended by corrupt **eunuchs**.[12] The situation worsened when the country was hit by famine and plague sparking a peasant rebellion led by the **Yellow Turbans**.

The Yellow Turbans were defeated by an Imperial General, **Cao Cao**, who eventually became the real power behind the Han throne. Upon Cao Cao's death in 220, his son, **Cao Pi** forced the last Han emperor to abdicate the throne and proclaimed himself to be the **Emperor of Wei** (or **Cao Wei**).

---

[10] The Chinese had been weaving silk fabric since at least 3000 B.C.. They maintained their monopoly on the silk industry by carefully guarding the secret of cultivating the mulberry trees on which silk worms fed and how the silk thread was spun, threatening execution for anyone who revealed the process.

[11] Paper is considered to be one of the Four Great Inventions of Ancient China along with the compass, gunpowder, and printing. The Chinese used paper toilet paper in the 6th century A.D. – many centuries before the rest of the world.

[12] Throughout much of China's history (until 1911) a class of castrated men held immense power and wealth. Eunuchs were originally hired to guard the quarters of the Emperors' wives and concubines. Since their genitalia had been removed, there was no risk of the eunuchs having sexual relations with the women and siring royal offspring. However, because they had free access to the royal family, they often became powerful and corrupt intermediaries between the rulers and administrators and, in some cases, even made decisions for the emperor himself.

THREE KINGDOMS PERIOD (220-280)

Despite their efforts, the new Wei emperors could not unify China. For the next four hundred years, China was engaged in a civil war among the three rival states of **Wei** (220-265) (in northern China), **Shu** (221-265) (the weakest kingdom, to the west) and **Wu** (221-280) (to the east).

JIN DYNASTY (265 – 420)

By 263, the Shu kingdom had been overpowered by the **Wei** and renamed **Jin**. Two years later, the Chancellor of the Kingdom of Wei, **Sima Yan**, took power from the Wei leader and proclaimed himself Emperor of the **Jin Dynasty**.[13] Fifteen years later, in 280, the Jin emperor defeated the Wu reunifying China and bringing the Three Kingdoms Period to an end.

In the early 4th century, the Jin were attacked in the north by nomadic, Turk-Mongolians from the **Xianbei** tribe [14] forcing tens of thousands of refugees to move to the sparsely populated southeast.

The invasion essentially split China into two cultural spheres with the north **Sixteen Kingdoms** [15] sinking into warfare and barbarianism and the southeast, reorganized as the **Eastern Jin Empire** (317-420),[16] becoming a comparatively peaceful, prosperous, cultural center that attracted merchants and **Buddhist** missionaries from Southeast Asia and India.

NORTHERN AND SOUTHERN DYNASTIES (420-581)

In 420, the **Eastern Jin Dynasty** was defeated by **Liu Song Dynasty** which was in turn overtaken by a series of short-lived dynasties including the **Liu Song Dynasty,** the **Southern Qi**, the **Liang Dynasty** and the **Chen Dynasty** (see box).

After the fall of the last of the Sixteen Kingdoms in 386, the north was dominated by the **Northern Wei Dynasty**, followed by the **Eastern Wei**, the **Western Wei**, **Northern Qi** and finally the **Northern Zhou**.

Initially, the northern steppe tribesmen maintained separate cultural identities from the Han in the south. Eventually, though, Chinese customs, dress, language and family names were adopted as well as the

Southern Dynasties
Liu song
Southern Qi
Liang
Chen
Northern Dynasties
Northern Wei
Eastern Wei
Western Wei
Northern Qi
Northern Zhou

---

[13] Upon his accession to the throne, Sima Yan became Emperor Wu of Jin (not to be confused with Emperor Wu of the Han Dynasty).

[14] The Xianbei were a confederation of non-Han people who lived in Manchuria and eastern Mongolia.

[15] Sixteen Kingdoms was the name given to the series of short-lived empires that ruled in northern China in the first half of the fourth century.

[16] The earlier Jin Dynasty (265-316) was henceforth called the "Western Jin Dynasty."

interest in Buddhism. Tens of thousands of Buddhist statues were built as a result – most impressively carved into the walls of the **Longmen Caves** near Luoyang – as well as pagodas (towers built to enshrine Buddhist scriptures and other sacred objects) and other holy structures.

SUI (581-618)

The north and south were finally reunited when **Yang Jian (Emperor Wen of Sui or Wendi)** defeated the last **Northern Zhou** emperor in 581, conquered the **Southern Chen Dynasty** and initiated a period of prosperity.

In order to strengthen cultural and economic ties between the north and the south, **Emperor Wen** ordered the construction of a 100-mile long canal to connect the Yellow and Yangtze Rivers.

Wen was succeeded by his son Yang, a tyrannical emperor known for his cruelty to his own people. Emperor Yang forced millions of peasants to work on the royal palace in the capital, **Luoyang**, and other engineering projects. Construction on the canal continued under Emperor Yang's rule and the **Grand Canal**, the longest man-made waterway in the world (larger than the Suez or Panama Canal) became the main artery in the country's transportation. But the accomplishment came at a high price – more than six million workers died as a result and the redirection of labor caused famine and desolation in the countryside. Emperor Yang's excesses brought about his own downfall in 618 when he was strangled by one of his own soldier.

TANG DYNASTY (618-907)

In Emperor Yang's place arose **Li Yuan**, one of Yang's generals who had joined the rebellion against the Sui emperor at the encouragement of his son **Li Shimin**. In 618, Li Yuan united China under the newly established **Tang Dynasty** and became **Emperor Gaozu**. Rule over the Tang Dynasty passed from Emperor Gaozu in 626 to his son, **Li Shimin** who then became known as **Emperor Taizong**.[17]

Emperor Taizong has historically been considered one of China's greatest leaders both because of his governance and because of his faithful adherence to the Confucian principles of benevolent leadership. In his reign, China enjoyed unparalleled prosperity and social order. Rice was cheap, taxes were low, there was little crime and the government was free of corruption.

China's borders during the Tang Dynasty stretched as far south as Vietnam,

---

[17] Chinese emperors were often known by a number of different names including the family name (considered too personal to utter when the emperor reigned), the reign title, honorifics (as in the "martial emperor" "Wudi"), temple names, and even posthumous names. Emperor Gaozu translates as "High Forefather." Taizong means "Great Ancestor" and is a common reign name.

northeast to Korea and northwest through Central Asia to the borders of Persia (Iran) after the Turk tribe, the **Gokturks**, were crushed. Even Tibet was brought into the Chinese fold when Emperor Taizong's niece married Tibet's leader (**Songtsan Gampo**) in 640 (see pg. 92).

The conquests allowed the Tang Emperors to rule over the whole Silk Road making travel along the trade route safer and easier. Diplomats, traders, scholars and priests journeyed from China throughout the world while merchants, artists and travelers arrived from Korea, Southeast Asia, Persia and the Arab world contributing to the exchange of East/West cultures by bringing exotic goods, artistic styles and different faiths from their homelands.

Chang' an (present-day Xi'an), the Tang capital and the eastern hub of the Silk Road, rivaled Rome as the world's most spectacular, cosmopolitan city in the pre-modern world boasting a population of more than a million people. To serve the diverse populace, Zoroastrian temples, Nestorian Christian churches and, from the mid 8th century onwards, Muslim mosques were erected in the city alongside other houses of worship.

Emperor Taizong was succeeded by his 9th son who was crowned **Emperor Gaozong** (r. 650-683). In 684, Gaozong was succeeded by his son **Zhongzong** who was followed by Zhongzong's younger brother **Ruizong** (r. 684-690). Actual rule over China for the next few decades, though, largely fell to **Empress Wu (Wu Zetian)** who had been Emperor Taizong's former concubine, became Gaozong's second wife, and was the mother of Emperors Zhongzong and Ruizong.[18]

Wu Zetian began her rise to power when her husband Gaozong fell ill.[19] Her influence increased after Gaozong's death when she served as the regent during the reign of her sons and culminated in 690 when Emperor Ruizong was forced to

Empress: The legal wife of the Emperor
Consort: The spouse of a monarch
Concubine: The second (or 3rd, 4th etc.), lesser wife or mistress. A concubine usually had fewer privileges and legal rights than a wife.
Dowager: Widow
Regent: One who rules when a monarch is too young or incapable of ruling.
Regnant: Ruler

---

[18] It was Empress Wu who deposed Zhongzong in favor of his more compliant brother Ruizong.

[19] Wu Zetian rose to the position of Empress after manipulating Gaozong into deposing his first wife. According to legend, Wu Zetian killed her own daughter and then accused the reigning empress of killing the child. As planned, the accusation caused the empress's downfall.

relinquish the throne making her the first and only female Regnant (see box on previous page) of China. Wu Zetian ruled the new Zhou Dynasty for fifteen years (690-705) under the title **Emperor Shengshen**.

Wu Zetian's rule has been viewed both negatively and positively by historians. Her critics focus on her ruthless quest for power that resulted in the death of three of her children and the dismissal of two emperors. She was said to have killed many officials who opposed her and encouraged others to secretly report on their rivals. She was also accused of inviting young men to her palace for her sexual pleasure. Those who viewed her positively deemed her an enlightened, attentive ruler who recognized and appointed capable men to govern the empire.

In 705, Wu Zetian was overthrown in a coup. Her son, former **Emperor Zhongzong** was restored to the throne followed briefly by Zhongzong's son **Chongmao** (710), former **Emperor Ruizong** (710-712) and then by his son, Wu's grandson, **Xuanzong** who seized the throne from his father (Emperor Ruizong) and introduced a second glorious period in China's history.

China's economy flourished under **Emperor Xuanzong** (r. 712-756) (known as the "Brilliant Emperor") and the people enjoyed an era of peace and cultural development. But the Emperor is most known for his deep love for his concubine, **Yang Guifei**, the beautiful daughter of a commoner. Xuanzong was so infatuated with the young concubine that he neglected the affairs of the empire in order to devote all his time to his beloved.

With the Emperor distracted, the court became progressively corrupt and extravagant provoking anger within the military. Discontent finally turned into revolt in 755. The rebels, led by the general **An Lushan,** took control of China's major cities and then captured the emperor and his concubine when they tried to flee. Because they blamed Yang Guifei for the enfeebled state of the empire, they forced her to commit suicide as the Emperor watched helplessly. The Emperor, overcome with grief, was powerless against the violent insurgents and died heartbroken in 762 while the **An Lushan Rebellion** (or **An Shi Rebellion**) continued.[20]

The Tang Empire continued to deteriorate under the rule of Xuanzong's ineffective and self-indulgent successors. Much of the dynasty's governance was taken over by the court's eunuchs while rebels and barbarian Uighurs, a powerful Turkish-speaking horde that had been invited to help defend the country from an onslaught of Tibetan tribes, ransacked China's cities. Eastern China was captured by rebels led by **Huang Chao** in 874 but the situation devolved into anarchy soon after.

---

[20] The uprising was called the "An Shi" Rebellion after the names of An Lushan and Shi Siming, his military commander. The turmoil left the country vulnerable to attack. In 763, even Chang'an, the Tang capital, was besieged by Tibet (see pg. 93).

FIVE DYNASTIES AND TEN STATES (907-960)

For the next fifty years, northern China was ruled by five combative dynasties while the south was governed by a dozen or so, short-lived but relatively stable regimes.

At the same time, a nomadic tribe called the **Khitans** [21] established a kingdom north of China in the Manchurian region that they called the **Liao Dynasty** (907-1125). In the 920s the Khitans expanded west forming an empire that would later threaten the Chinese.

SONG DYNASTY (960-1279)

In the year 960, a military general from the last of the northern Five Dynasties reunified northern China under the **Song Empire** becoming **Emperor Taizu** (r. 960-970). The unification of most of the former territories of the Tang period was completed by 979 under his brother **Taizong**.

The emperors of the Song Dynasty were more cultivated than at any other period in China's history. They fostered a culturally-rich society of poets, philosophers, intellectuals and artists. (Chinese porcelain or "fine China" reached its highest quality during the

Song Dynasty). But while the community flourished artistically, socially[22] and intellectually, it was becoming impoverished due to tributes paid to barbarians to keep them safely at bay in the north.

For the first 100 years or so, the Song were under almost constant attack from the **Khitans**, a nomadic group that dominated Manchuria and established the **Liao Dynasty**, and then the **Jurchens**, who, in 1115 established the **Jin Dynasty**. In 1125, the Jin absorbed the Khitans and, two years later, took the Song capital of Bianliang (present-day Kaifeng). The Jin then captured **Emperor Huizong**[23] and his son (who had become **Emperor Qinzong** when his father abdicated). But **Prince Kang**, younger brother of the captured emperor escaped to the south

---

[21] The name "Khitan" was the source of the name "Cathay" which was used as an alternative name for China by the English (e.g. Cathay Pacific Airlines).

[22] Under Emperor Shenzong (r. 1067-1085), Wang Anshi, a political statesman and poet, abolished the corvee - a system that allowed feudal lords to compel their subjects to do labor (for example working on roads) in lieu of paying taxes. He also reformed the civil service exams by banning nepotism and putting more emphasis on the testing of proficiency in economics and geography.

[23] Emperor Huizon (r. 1100-1135), one of the most renowned Song emperors, was a musician, painter, calligrapher and poet who compiled a collection of more than 6,000 imperial paintings.

becoming **Emperor Gaozong** (r. 1127-1162) of the new regime **Southern Song**.

The Song reassembled in the south in the most fertile lands around the Yangtze River using it as their line of defense against the Jin to the north. Under the rule of **Gaozong**, the Southern Song flourished from 1127-1279 artistically and economically. The port cities of Guangzhou, Xiamen and Quanzhou prospered as international commerce expanded along the "Silk Road of the Sea" as did the Chinese shipbuilding industry. The Chinese led the world in nautical expertise (the first navigational compass was used on Chinese ships at this time). Paper money came into circulation due to a copper shortage, and gunpowder was used in war for the first time.

Until the 13th century, the Chinese were able to resist the **Uighurs** (7th and 8th centuries), the **Khitans (Liao Dynasty)** and **Jurchens (Jin Dynasty)** on their northern borders by offering them lucrative tributes. But they could not defend themselves against the Mongols who wiped out the Jin in 1234.

YUAN (1279-1842)
The Mongols first emerged as a tribe in the 12th century as vassals to the Khitans and the Jurchens. Under the leadership of **Temudjin**, better known as **Genghis Khan** ("Almighty Emperor"), though, the Khitans and Jurchens fell under Mongol control. Joined with other Central Eurasian nomadic groups, the Mongols eventually became the largest contiguous empire the world had ever seen.[24]

In 1211, with help from the Song, the Mongols invaded the **Jin** in northern China and, seven years later, conducted violent campaigns across Asia to Iran [25] resulting in the deaths of millions of people. After Genghis Khan died in 1227, rule over the Mongolian Empire was passed to his third son **Ogedai** with his other sons assuming leadership of the western Mongol regions.

The Mongol Empire broke into four independent states or "Khanates"[26] with Genghis Khan's grandson, **Kublai Khan** (1215-1294) ruling over the Mongolian homeland (the "Great Khanate") north of China.

In 1271 Kublai Khan adopted the dynastic name **Yuan**[27] and declared **Dadu** (present-day **Beijing**) the capital. After decades of wars, the Mongols finally defeated the Southern Song in 1279 uniting China and incorporating Mongolia and Siberia.

---

[24] The Mongolian Empire covered more than 20% of the world's total area.

[25] The Mongols under Genghis Khan's grandson, Hulagu, invaded Iran and, in 1258, captured Baghdad, the capital of the Muslim Caliphate. The Mongols of Iran, Iraq, Afghanistan, Turkey and surrounding countries set up the Ilkhanid dynasty and eventually converted to Islam.

[26] The four Khanates included the Ogedei Khanate, the Chagatai Khanate of Central Asia (Turkestan, Uzbekistan, Turkmenistan etc.), the Ilkhanate (Iran, Iraq etc.), and the Golden Horde which, at its peak, penetrated deep into Europe.

[27] The use of the name Yuan, a Chinese word, was intended to help the Mongols present themselves as heirs to the Chinese Song Dynasty.

Kublai Khan's deep mistrust of the Han Chinese coupled with the Mongols' sense of superiority resulted in a discriminatory government. Chinese naval techniques, the Chinese use of gunpowder and the Chinese system of government bureaucracy were all adopted by the new overlords. But the Khans reserved high posts for Mongols or other non-Chinese individuals (the **Four Class System**)[28] and Mongol customs, dress and language were mandated.

Trade opened significantly between the West and East through the chain of political entities or "Khanates" that were ruled by the Mongol Khans. Foreign travelers, ambassadors and religious men were lured by the promise of tax-free trading and unfettered travel throughout China and were warmly welcomed by the Yuan rulers and traders. (The Han Chinese, by comparison, were forbidden to move freely about the country or engage in external trade.)

Perhaps the most famous foreigner feted by Kublai Khan was the Venetian traveler **Marco Polo** who recorded detailed accounts of his journeys to China in the book <u>**Il Milione**</u>, known also as "**The Travels of Marco Polo**."[29] The stories about the riches to be found in the Far East greatly inspired European visitors and explorers like **Christopher Columbus** to make the journey to Asia.

The trade links with Europe, Persia and the Arab world enriched the Chinese people culturally and economically and played a great role in China's advancement. Scientific books from foreign countries were brought in and translated, Arabic numerals and mathematical methods were introduced, western medicines and

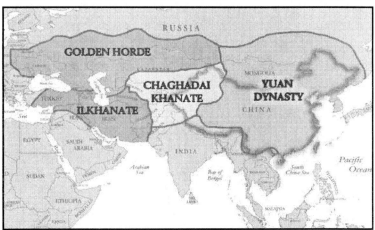

---

[28] The Mongols instituted a Four Class tiered-system of power and influence. At the top were the Mongolian people. Next were the Semu or "colored-eyed" people (Europeans as well as Arabs, Persians, Tibetans and other foreigners). Han Chinese from the north were third on the list followed by Han from the south.

[29] Marco Polo's account of the exquisite summer palace at Shangdu (in present-day Inner Mongolia) was immortalized as "Xanadu" in the poem "Kublai Khan" by Samuel T. Coleridge.

medical treatments began to supplement traditional Chinese practices and developments were made in agriculture, the handicraft industry and other areas.

But the success of the Yuan Dynasty could only be maintained to such a degree under its founder, Kublai Khan. The Yuan emperors taking power after Kublai Khan's death in 1294 were less competent. The ruling class was corrupt. And the government was crippled by power struggles.

The Han Chinese, meanwhile, were beginning to rise up in resentment over the political economic discrimination engendered by the Four Class System. Over-taxed peasants rebelled over the disparity between the extravagant lifestyles enjoyed by Yuan ruling class and their own impoverished states. Intellectuals complained of oppression. And merchants and consumers protested over high inflation caused by the Yuan's practice of over-printing paper money. Making matters worse, the country suffered a series of natural disasters – in particular a massive Yellow River flood that destroyed farms and put hundreds of thousands of peasants to work repairing the dikes.

The rebellion that finally toppled the Yuan dynasty was instigated by an esoteric Buddhist sect that had been forced underground by the Mongols. The **White Lotus Society** became a national resistance force in the mid-14th century under the lead of **Zhu Yuanzhang**, a poor peasant and Buddhist monk who left his monastery to join the rebellion. Known as the **Red Turbans** (because they donned red headwear and flew red flags) the rebels captured Jianking (present-day Nanjing) in 1356. Twelve years later they entered the Mongol capital of Beijing forcing the Mongols to retreat north. Upon Zhu Yuanzhang's success, the former monk took the title of **Emperor Hongwu** ("vast military") and founded the ethnically Han Chinese **Ming Dynasty**.

MING DYNASTY (1368-1644)

The despised rule of the alien Mongolians and their preferential treatment for non-Han Chinese left a deep impression on the populace. After the Mongols were overthrown, the Chinese rejected all foreign influences and adopted a policy of isolation that lasted into the 20th century. The government focused its attention inward improving agriculture in order to create self-sufficient communities, fixing and maintaining the dikes of the Yellow and Yangtze Rivers, lowering taxes and taking measures to prevent future famines. Trade was seen as a dishonorable occupation and, to keep the population in place, travel, even from village to village, was discouraged. In order to defend the country against the Mongols, who continued to threaten the Chinese from the north, the Ming emperors rebuilt and reinforced the **Great Wall**, a further symbol of their insularity.

The distrust of outsiders also permeated the government. Fearing conspiracies and rebellion, **Emperor Hongwu** (r. 1368-1398) took full autocratic rule and purged educated elites, Yuan-friendly civil servants and other critics. He also employed a secret police force that was responsible for the deaths of tens of thousands of people in the three decades of his rule.

Chinese isolation briefly lessened under the rule of **Emperor Yongle** (r. 1403-1424) who oversaw a cultural and economic revival in the early 1400s.

In order to keep a closer eye on the Mongols, Yongle moved the Ming capital from Nanjing to **Beijing** (then known as **Peking**) where he constructed the historic **Forbidden City,** a palatial residence built exclusively for the emperor and his family.

Unlike his predecessors, Yongle greatly respected scholarly pursuits. During his reign, he commissioned thousands of writers to compile the biggest and earliest encyclopedias the world had ever seen. In order to gather more information, Yongle also ordered his favorite eunuch, **Zheng He**, a Muslim from the Hui ethnic group, to command a fleet of 63 ships to sail across the Indian Ocean on a massive tributary expedition. The Imperial navy visited countries in Southeast Asia, East Asia, Africa, southern India, Ceylon (Sri Lanka) and the Middle East expanding the influence of the Ming Dynasty. The expeditions earned China great prestige as the world's greatest naval power and increased international desire for Chinese tea, silk, Ming porcelain, lacquer ware, paintings and other Chinese goods.

But the expeditions were halted suddenly after Yongle's death in 1424.

Yongle's successors felt the cost of such extravagant missions were unnecessary, especially since the ships were commanded by a eunuch (not a general). They also felt that exposure to foreign luxuries would eventually lead to the dynasty's downfall. Consequently, all the records documenting the journeys were burned and shipbuilding laws were implemented restricting the size of

The Forbidden City

vessels. All private maritime trade was forbidden under the *hai jin* ("ocean forbidden") ban that remained in place until the middle of the 16th century forcing traders to go underground. Without Ming ships patrolling the seas, Japanese pirates (*wokou*) had free reign to wreak havoc along China's coastal cities.

Where the Chinese left off the Europeans took over, embarking on an Age of Discovery that saw the great voyages of Italian explorers **Christopher Columbus** and **John Cabot**, the Portuguese explorers **Fernando Magellan** and **Vasco de Gama** and others.

Foreign trade with China was re-instigated somewhat in the mid-1500s when the country began to use silver as currency. Silver, as well as maize, sweet potatoes and other crops, was imported from the Spanish territories in the **New World** and, in return for their help battling Japanese pirates, the **Portuguese** (who united with Spain in 1580) were permitted to establish a trade colony at **Macau** (which would be administered by Portugal for the next four hundred years). From their trade post off the coast of south China, the Portuguese enjoyed privileged trade relations with China and monopolized commerce between China and India, Spain, the Philippines and Mexico until trade was opened to all countries in 1685.

As China grew wealthier in the 16th century, so did the emperors who enjoyed extravagant luxuries within the palatial setting of the 8,000-room **Forbidden City**. Affairs of the state were increasingly taken over by the eunuchs who frequently formed into feuding cliques and engaged in nepotism and corruption.

In the north, meanwhile, **Nurhaci** (r. 1616-1626), a chieftain of a Jurchen tribe was building a great power that would eventually bring the Ming Dynasty to an end. In the 1580s, Nurhaci began to unify Jurchen bands in order to avenge the death of his father and grandfather, both killed by a rival Jurchen chief. By 1616, he had created an empire which was dubbed the **Later Jin Dynasty** (after the empire founded by Jurchens in 1115) with Nurhaci presiding as Khan.

Nurhaci's son, **Huang Taiji** (r. 1626-1643) took over where his father left off. After consolidating the Later Jin Empire he renamed it the **Qing Dynasty**[30] in 1636 and changed the name of the Jurchens to **Manchus**. Taiji, like his father, had great ambitions to rule over China and incorporated Han Chinese, albeit in minor roles, into the Ming-styled Qing bureaucracy to facilitate the takeover. By the time of his death, the Qing controlled the region that would later be known as **Manchuria**, they had invaded Korea, at that time the **Joseon Dynasty**, and had penetrated deep into Mongolia. But, just months

[30] Sharing his father's goal of taking over China, Taiji reasoned that the Manchus would be more readily accepted as leaders if they didn't share the same name as their enemies, the Jurchen people, who had ruled Northern China from 1115-1234 during the Song period and called their reign the Jin Dynasty.

before Huang Taiji would realize his dream of penetrating China, he died. Since Taiji's five- year-old son, **Shunzhi**, was too young to rule, command over the Manchus passed to a regent, Shunzhi's half-brother **Dorgon**.

QING DYNASTY (1644-1911)

Turmoil within the Ming Dynasty left the rulers powerless to defend the Empire from the **Manchu Qing** army assembled on their northern borders.

In 1644, the leader of a peasant uprising, **Li Zicheng**, had successfully occupied the Ming capital at Beijing (Peking). Using the ensuing chaos to their advantage, the Manchus manipulated a guard at a Great Wall pass fifty miles from Beijing into opening the gates letting the Manchu army through. Realizing defeat, the last Ming Emperor **Chongzhen** (r. 1628-1644) hanged himself. The Manchus swiftly expelled Li Zicheng and took over the city.

Until the young Manchu emperor **Shunzhi** came of age seven years later, de facto rule over the new Manchu Qing Dynasty was in the hands of the regent **Dorgon**.

Almost immediately after taking power, Dorgon enacted one of the most hated directives in the Qing era, the **"Queue Order,"** forcing all Han Chinese men to adopt the Manchu hair style (shaving the head to the temples and wrapping the rest in a long braid [or queue, French for pigtail]), or face death. The order met stiff resistance by the Chinese who believed, as Confucius had taught them, that hair was a gift from one's parents and should not be cut. The decree was intended to symbolically force the Chinese to submit to the Manchu rulers and to identify rebels. In fact, hundreds of thousands of Chinese men who refused to observe the law were massacred.

The Manchu also tried to outlaw foot-binding (the Chinese custom of breaking a young girl's feet at her soles and binding the toes under the arch of the foot making the feet tiny). Since a young girl's marriage prospects depended on her having "lotus" feet the Chinese would not give up this practice.

Like the Mongols of the Yuan Dynasty, the Manchus maintained their own customs and forbade intermarriage between Manchus and Han Chinese. Unlike the Mongols, though, the Manchus established a dual-government, employing both a Manchu and a Chinese civil servant to hold dual, equal positions and having separate Han and Manchu units in the military.

When Dorgon died in 1651 **Shunzhi** began his official rule. During his short reign (Shunzhi died in 1661 from smallpox) the Qing Emperor adopted most of Dorgon's policies and continued to subdue rebellious Ming-sympathizers. In 1653, Shunzhi also invited the spiritual and political leader of the Tibetans, the fifth **Dalai Lama**, to court in part to help control the last of the Mongols.[31] The Dalai Lama agreed to become the spiritual guide of the Manchu emperors in exchange for patronage and protection. (See pg. 95)

In observance of the arrangement, Shunzhi's successor, Qing **Emperor Kangxi** (r. 1662-1722) fought the **Dzungar Mongols** when they attacked Tibet in 1717. In 1750 the Manchus suppressed a rebellion by a Tibetan chief and, in the late 18th century, they defeated invading **Nepalese Gurkhas**. In 1725, the Manchus appointed resident ambassadors or "high officials" (*ambasa*) to tend to Manchu interests in Tibet but the actual extent of Qing suzerainty over Tibet is still debated.

Having established peaceful relations along China's western border, Emperor Kangxi began to focus on the Russians, who had begun to make incursions into China from the north, and the Ming-loyalist rebels who were attacking China from **Formosa** (present-day **Taiwan**). After successfully defeating the Russians in the 1689, Kangxi signed the **Treaty of Nerchinsk** extending China's border to the Stanovoy Mountains.[32]

In 1683, Kangxi's armies also defeated the **Kingdom of Tungning**, a pro-Ming/anti-Qing kingdom based in Taiwan that was founded by the former military leader **Koxinga**[33] in 1662. The victorious Qing ruled Taiwan for the next 200 years. (See pg. 101)

In the course of Kangxi's 60-year rule, China had grown to its greatest height of power since the early Ming Dynasty, in part because Kangxi courted European Jesuits who introduced the Chinese to the use of telescopes, trigonometry, mapmaking, Western methods of astronomy, hydraulics and other Western sciences. Earlier, **Johann Adam Schall**, a German Jesuit missionary, had even become a counselor to Emperor Shunzhi and helped modify the Chinese calendar (which incorporated elements of the lunar and solar calendar).

---

31 The Tibetans and Mongols shared a religion (Tibetan Buddhism) and both observed the authority of the Lamas (Buddhist leaders). Tibetans and Mongols were also politically connected in 1249 although the Tibetans maintained their own government and culture.

32 In 1858, the Manchu were forced to cede the region between the Amur River and the Stanovoy to Russia (Treaty of Aigun).

33 Koxinga, the son of a Chinese pirate and a Japanese woman, was considered a hero by the Chinese because he expelled the Dutch colonists from Taiwan after 38 years of occupation.

IMPERIALISM

The Jesuits, with hopes of converting vast populations of the country to Christianity,[34] like all foreigners, had arrived in China through the Portuguese port colony of **Macau**. Until the 1600s, the Portuguese maintained a monopoly on all trade with China because of their control of the port and due to China's isolationist restrictions on foreign entry into the mainland. Their privileged position ended in 1685 when the Emperor abandoned the link between tribute status and trade, opening commerce to all countries.[35]

Rivals to the Portuguese (who were by then having trouble managing their overstretched empire) flocked to the region. The first to arrive was the **Dutch East India Company,** the richest private trading company in the 17th century. The Dutch were then followed by the British and French who were hoping to take advantage of the great international demand for oriental goods: tea, silk and porcelain ("fine china").

In order to prevent the spread of alien ideas, the Qing regime strictly confined trade to the region around Macau. According to the **Canton System** (in place from 1760 to 1842) foreigners were forbidden to deal directly with civilians and had to conduct all their business under the supervision of the Chinese merchant guild called the **Cohong**. Outsiders were also forbidden to learn the Chinese language or travel inland.

Foreign trade expanded greatly at the end of 18th and beginning of the 19th centuries, especially with the conclusion of the 1803-1815 Napoleonic Wars. Along with the growing international exchange came an unquenchable appetite for Chinese products – an appetite that wasn't matched by Chinese interest in Western goods. Rather than bartering silk, tea and porcelain for Western items that wouldn't sell in the Chinese market, the Chinese traders preferred payment in silver.

This arrangement wasn't satisfactory to Western companies who saw their stashes of precious silver bullion quickly become depleted.

Initially, the **British East India Company** tried to break the trade imbalance by sending a Chinese-speaking representative to petition Qing Emperor **Qianlong**. Rather than taking action, though, the Emperor arrested the representative for learning Chinese and sailing to northern ports. British **King George III** tried again in 1793 by sending a mediator (**Lord Macartney**) to the Qing Court laden with gifts that were intended to exhibit the West's advances in art and manufac-

[34] Italian Jesuit Matteo Ricci attempted to show the Chinese how the teachings of Confucius were consistent with the Christian idea of a Creator God who created man in his own image. He also tried to convince the Chinese to reject Buddhism, Daoism and polygamy among other things,

[35] Until the 1600s, the Chinese had developed a tributary system. Tributary states (such as Korea, Japan and Vietnam) were granted exclusive, imperially-regulated, trading rights in return for their submission and allegiance to China in the same way that Confucianism dictated that a son should defer to his father.

turing deemed a "tribute from Britain." The Qing Emperor wasn't impressed.

In a last and devious attempt to break the Chinese traders' advantage, the **British East India Company** began to flood the market with **opium**, a highly addictive narcotic cheaply produced in the British colony of India.[36] The plan worked. The demand for opium skyrocketed as the population became addicted to the drug and China's supply of silver disappeared into British coffers.

In response, the Qing government banned the import of opium and, in 1839, terminated trade with Britain all together. From the British perspective, this action amounted to a declaration of war.

OPIUM WAR

For the next two years, the British navy, at its peak of development, shelled and then captured China's southern coastal cities. The outdated Chinese military couldn't compete with the far superior firepower of the British Royal Navy forcing the Qing Emperor to surrender in 1842 and sign a treaty.

Among the terms of the resulting **Treaty of Nanjing**, the Chinese were required to open four new ports to unrestricted trade, pay large indemnities, abolish the **Canton System**, and cede **Hong Kong Island** and **Kowloon** to Great Britain "in perpetuity" (the **New Territories** were later "leased" to the British for 99 years. See pg. 70)

After a series of minor incidents in the region (including an attempt by Chinese bakers to poison Europeans in Hong Kong), a **second Opium War** broke out in 1857.

This time, the defeated Chinese were forced to open up ten new ports, allow the British, French, Russians and Americans to station **legations** (small embassies) in the previously closed city of Beijing and allow foreigners to travel to the interior of China. The 1858 **Treaty of Tientsin** also legalized the opium trade, committed the Chinese to hand over millions of *taels* (one *tael* is equivalent to around 40 grams) of silver in reparation payments, and obliged the Chinese to grant Christians the right to own property and evangelize.

Humiliation over the defeat by foreigners, the subsequent "**unequal treaties**" and the economic hardship of high taxes that befell the country to pay the victors added fuel to existing popular discontent with the Manchu government.

TAIPING REBELLION (1850)

Among the many uprisings quelled by the Qing Emperors was one led by an ethnically Hakka (see footnote pg. 104) Christian convert who claimed to be

---

[36] Britain assumed complete administrative control over India and present-day Pakistan and Bangladesh in 1858 (called the British Raj Period) after progressively gaining economic and political influence in the region through the activities of the British East India Company.

the brother of Jesus. **Hong Xiuquan**, and the subjects of his **Heavenly Kingdom of Great Peace** planned to overthrow the Manchu government and institute social reforms in China including outlawing foot binding, equality of the sexes (even allowing women to fight alongside men), outlawing opium, gambling and the sale of slaves, socializing land and replacing all local religions with Christianity. Thirty million people in southern China had joined the rebellion before it was brutally put down by the Qing government with the help of French and British forces. Tens of millions of people were killed or starved to death in the course of one of the bloodiest uprisings in history.

Other uprisings, including rebellions by Muslims in the late 1800s (called the **Dungan Revolts** or **Panthay Rebellion**) protesting discrimination against the **Hui** people and other Chinese Muslims,[37] also ended in massacres of millions of people. (See pg. ????)

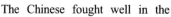

The **French** took advantage of the Qinq armies' preoccupation with the rebellions, by attempting to annex the northern part of Vietnam (**Tonkin**) in order to bypass the coastal ports and complete an overland trade route from their protectorate of Cambodia to southern China.[38]

The Chinese fought well in the **Sino-French War** of 1883-1885 but had to redirect troops towards the north to prevent the impending Japanese incursion into Korea. The French advances were successful. They took over Annam, Chochin China and Tonkin (which together make up present-day Vietnam) along with Laos and Cambodia establishing the French colony of **Indochina**.

SELF-STRENGTHENING MOVEMENT

The Opium Wars, rebellions and contact with the modernized armies of the West prompted the Qing regime to make some changes. From the late 1870s to the 1890s, the Manchu regime embarked on a "**Self-Strengthening Movement**" which attempted to combine Western technology with Confucian principles. Foreign language schools were opened as a result and Western sciences were studied. Students were sent to study abroad and some diplomatic practices were adopted. The Chinese military was also improved.

---

[37] Many of the Muslim survivors fled to neighboring countries (Thailand, Laos, Burma [Myanmar] and the Muslim regions of Imperial Russia [Kazakhstan and Kyrgyzstan]) establishing Chinese communities that still exist today.

[38] The French, who had allied with the British against China during the Opium Wars, also hoped to combat anti-Christian persecution and protect French Catholic missionaries in the area.

But most of the reforms fell short of expectations. Other reforms, especially those intended to improve the military, were sabotaged by corruption. The attempt to modernize was minimal compared to the rapid development taking place in Japan.

SINO-JAPANESE WAR (1897)

After two centuries of seclusion, the Japanese reemerged onto the world scene in the late 19th century. A series of reforms collectively called the **Meiji Restoration** had transformed Japan from a backwards feudal society into a prominent military power.[39]

In order to defend their newly developed empire from Western imperialism, the Japanese regime created a "line of advantage" beyond its borders. If a foreign power was to take hold of the **Korean Peninsula** to the immediate west of Japan, it was reasoned, Japan itself would be at risk. Korea, which was under Chinese sovereignty at the time, would be a less risky neighbor if it was under Japanese administration or operating as an independent country.

In 1884, the Japanese helped reformers in Korea stage a coup against the Korean royal family. Conservatives who supported the Korean royals and favored a relationship with neighboring China staged a counter-coup with help from China. By 1894, the civil conflict had escalated into war between Japan and China.

Despite the attempts to improve China's firepower through the **Self-Strengthening Movement**, China's badly equipped and demoralized fleet was easily defeated by the newly modernized Japanese Navy.

---

[39] Beginning in 1867, Japan made a number of changes in order to free itself from the domination of the imperialistic Europeans and Americans. In 1868 the Meiji emperor was restored as head of Japan (although real power remained in the hands of a ruling clique). A parliament or Diet was established. Religious freedom, compulsory education and equality between the social classes was instituted. Economic emphasis shifted from agriculture to industry and great reforms were made in the military (which was modeled after the Prussian Army and British Navy).

After taking Korea, the Japanese head-
ed to **Port Arthur** (home of the
Beiyang fleet), massacred tens of
thousands of Chinese servicemen and
civilians, and overtook the **Liaodong
Peninsula**. In March 1895, the
Japanese invaded and occupied
Taiwan and the **Pescadores** Islands.

A month later, the Chinese were
forced to sign the **Treaty of
Shimonoseki** recognizing Korea's
independence, ceding Taiwan and the Pescadores Islands to Japan "in perpetuity"
and also ceding the **Liaodong Peninsula** (later handed to Russia by Germany
and France).[40] On top of the indemnities already owed to European countries, the
Chinese were obliged to pay Japan 200 million *taels* of silver in reparations.

The Sino-Japanese War demonstrated Japan's new status as a regional power
on par with the West. China, on the other hand, had lost the bulk of its naval
fleet and saw chunks of territory disappear into foreign hands. The Germans
acquired the **Jiaochow Bay** (including the cities of **Qingdao** [Tsingtao][41]
and **Kiaochow**), the British acquired **Weihai Port** in 1905 to counter
Russia's presence at Port Arthur, and France annexed Guangzhouwan in
south China in 1898 to compete with British Hong Kong.

EMPRESS DOWAGER CIXI (Virtual Ruler 1882-1908)

From the 1860s until the early 20th century, China's government was dominated by an uneducated former concubine who began exercising de facto
power when her husband, **Emperor Xiafeng,** became incapacitated. Soon
after his death in 1861, **Empress Dowager Cixi** became the regent, effectively ruling on behalf of her 5-year-old son,
Emperor Tongzhi, until he was old enough to
govern on his own. When Tongzhi died of smallpox in 1875, she presided over the rule of her 4-
year old nephew, **Emperor Guangxu** as regent.

Some historians have portrayed Cixi as a capable
ruler whose strength derived from her ability to
seek out and appoint talented administrators.
Others claim that her despotic rule and deep resist-

---

[40] For fear that Japan's ownership of the Peninsula would interfere with European trade to
Beijing, Russia, France and Germany forced Japan to give up the Liaodong Peninsula in
return for 30 million *taels* of silver to be paid by the Chinese. Russia was granted a 25-year
lease on the Liaodong Peninsula as a result of the 1895 "Triple Intervention." Russia's presence in the region eventually became the cause of the 1904-1905 Russo-Japanese War.
[41] The Germans founded the Tsingtao Brewery in that city in 1903.

ance to reform was responsible for the eventual fall of the Empire. Indeed, the Empress regularly dismissed, imprisoned or killed her critics.

HUNDRED DAYS REFORM

Emperor Guangxu began his rule at the conclusion of China's terrible defeat in the Sino-Japanese war. More reform-minded than his aunt, Guangxu attempted to make some serious changes. In 1895, the Qing armies were modernized according to Western standards with the first of the upgraded "new armies" (later renamed the **Beiyang Army**) emerging in December under the command of **Yuan Shikai**, an ally of Empress Cixi.

Other reforms included the creation of a modern education system that focused less on Confucian studies and more on science and math, the modernization of the exam system, rapid industrialization, the introduction of capitalistic principles and, most significantly, the introduction of an elected, constitutional government overseen by a hereditary monarch.

Cixi and her supporters considered the reforms too radical and, fearing a conspiracy and the collusion of the Japanese, ended the movement 104 days later (hence the name **Hundred Days Reform**) by putting her nephew under house arrest and executing the principle advocates. The inability of the Qing regime to reform itself from within would later compel rebels to save China by overthrowing the regime.

BOXER REBELLION

Piece by piece, China was being engulfed by foreign powers, from the loss of Hong Kong to Britain after the First Opium War in 1842 to the occupation of the Jiaochow Bay by the Germans in 1898. China's naval fleet was nearly destroyed by the Japanese and indemnity payments were financially breaking China.

Popular resentment had been growing since the 1830s but the regimes successful and brutal suppression of all open rebellions forced disgruntled Chinese to go underground congregating in secret societies. Anger that might otherwise have been directed at the Manchu regime was targeted instead against the "foreign devils" and their Chinese Christian convert collaborators.

In the Shandong Province, a secret society arose called the "**Righteous and Harmonious Fists**," or "**Boxers**" in the West (because of members involvement in the martial arts) in opposition to the foreign domination of China. Their grievances included the annexation of Qingdao (in Jiaochow) by the Germans and Weihei by the British, the construction of foreign railroads, the proliferation of churches and roving Christian missionaries.

Initially, the Chinese government tried to subdue the Boxers' violent rampage. They massacred missionaries and Chinese Christians and destroyed foreign property. But when they dropped their anti-government stance, Cixi embraced them – even after receiving warnings by Western governments that they would deploy military forces to protect their citizens if the Qing government didn't curb the violence.

By May 1900, the Boxers, now joined by some members of the Imperial army, began killing foreign diplomats and attacking the foreign legations in Beijing. In response, the Europeans and Japanese united to form an eight-nation military alliance against the Boxers. After a couple of battles, the foreign forces occupied Beijing and pursued Boxer sympathizers throughout China.

Under the mounting pressure, the Empress Dowager agreed to abolish the Boxer Society in early 1901 and signed the **Boxer Protocol** a few months later promising to pay 450 million *taels* of silver in reparation.

More than 18,000 Chinese Catholic and Protestant Christians and foreigners had been killed by the Boxers in the course of the rebellion and more than 50,000 Chinese civilians accused of being Boxers were executed by foreign troops when the violence had ended.

The defeat was another crushing blow to the regime. Making a last-ditch effort to reform once again, the regime sent two official missions abroad, began construction on modern colleges and discontinued the imperial examination system. The Empress Dowager even permitted the government to begin drafting a constitution in 1906 and establish provincial legislatures.

In 1908 Empress Dowager Cixi had the former emperor Guangxu executed and placed two-year old **Puyi** on the throne. The next day Cixi died a natural death. A provincial legislature was established and plans were made to create a national parliament in 1910. But the reforms had come too late and were rejected by conservatives. Popular Anti-Manchu/Anti-Qing sentiments prevailed bringing the dynastic regime to an end in 1911.

PUYI
After his formal abdication in 1912 after the **Xinhai Revolution,** China's "last emperor" Puyi and his court were permitted to continue living in the northern half of the Forbidden City. For a brief time in 1917, Puyi was restored to power by warlord general **Zhang Xun** but he was deposed again twelve days later. In 1924, Puyi was expelled from Beijing and relocated in Tianjin.

Eight years later, Puyi was installed by the Japanese as the ruler of **Manchukuo**, a state in Manchuria and eastern Inner Mongolia created by former Qing officials and administered by Imperial Japan (see pg. 34).

After the Japanese were defeated at the end of World War II, Puyi was captured by the Soviet Red Army and sentenced to ten years in a rehabilitation prison. He lived as an ordinary citizen in Beijing until 1964 when he was made a member of the Chinese People's Political Consultative Conference - a post he held until his death in 1967.

MODERN HISTORY

By the turn of the 20th century, it was clear that change was necessary in order to save China from being engulfed by Japan and the West. But opinions differed over the type and extent of change to be implemented.

Supporters of the Manchu Qing regime attempted to create a more modern constitutional monarchy. By May 1911, a prime minister had been appointed and a cabinet created. But most of its members were ethnically Manchu or came directly from the family of the emperor.

Conservatives who opposed Manchu dominance in the government advocated a return to the ethnically Han values of the Ming Dynasty.

The most powerful reformists, primary among them anti-Qing activist **Sun Yat-Sen** and the members of his organization, the **Tongmenghui** (Revolutionary Alliance), believed that the Chinese dynastic system needed to be overhauled completely by way of revolution.

SUN YAT-SEN

Often deemed the "father of modern China," Sun Yat-Sen was born in southern China near Macau. At 13 he moved to Honolulu, Hawaii where he was exposed to Christianity and Western values. While in the United States, Sun Yat-Sen created the **Revive China Society** dedicated to revitalizing China by expelling foreigners and establishing a unified government.

In 1895 in Guangzhou, Sun Yat-sen attempted to stage his first uprising against the Qing Empire. The rebellion failed and Sun was forced to flee, first to Japan (which later became the base for his revolutionary activity) and then to Europe where he studied Western political trends. Two years later, Sun penned **Three Principles of the People: Nationalism, Democracy and the People's Welfare**. In his doctrine, Sun Yat-Sen advocated the overthrow of the minority Manchu government, China's liberation from foreign domination, the creation of a government elected by the people and the abolition of social exploitation (particularly industrial capitalism and the dominance of powerful landlords).

Sun Yat-Sen attracted a significant following throughout Asia, Europe, Canada and the United States, especially among Chinese citizens living or studying abroad. [42] His popularity and his coffers grew even more rapidly after it was reported in the foreign press that Sun Yat-Sen had been kidnapped in Britain by members of the Qing-controlled Chinese Embassy. (He was released due to international pressure).

---

[42] Chinese expatriates still revere Sun Yat-Sen as the father of the Republic of China. Statues of the famous revolutionary today grace squares in Chinatowns and other Chinese enclaves worldwide.

In 1905, Sun Yat-Sen created the **Tongmenghui** or **Revolutionary Alliance**, a secret society that united his **Revive China Society** with other revolutionary groups and disenfranchised Chinese (for example reformers who had fled China after the Hundred Days Reform). Between 1906 and 1911, the Revolutionary Alliance made numerous attempts to bring about a revolution, but it was grassroots revolts that sparked the insurgency that finally ended 4,000 years of dynastic rule.

Wuchang Rebellion

Much to the dismay of local leaders, after the death of **Empress Cixi** in 1908, the Manchu Qing court was run by inefficient and incompetent administrators who expended more energy trying to maintain central authority than developing the constitutional rule of the fledgling parliament. Therefore, when the Manchu government tried to take over control of the railway system, many of the local provinces (Sichuan in particularly) began to angrily protest. The uprising provoked simmering anti-Qing feelings in the city of **Wuhan** (in the Wuchang district, Hubei province) where local revolutionaries successfully seized the government's ammunitions depot and took control of the city. News of the success in Wuhan spread to other regions where similar uprisings took place.

By the end of 1911, nearly every province in China south of the Yangtze River had declared its independence from Qing rule and the revolutionaries, assembled by the **Revolutionary Alliance**, had established the **Provisional Republican Government** in Nanjing with Sun Yat-Sen sworn in as President.

Without military strength, though, the Revolutionary Alliance had no hope of reunifying China or establishing national control. The strongest military in the land, the **Beiyang Army** commanded by **Yuan Shikai**, was still under Qing authority giving the imperial regime the power to quash the revolts. The revolution could only be successful if Yuan Shikai, with his loyal army, could be persuaded to switch sides. He was finally seduced when the revolutionaries promised to appoint him leader of the republican government if he could get the emperor to step down.

Under Yuan's pressure, the child emperor, **Puyi**, was forced to abdicate on February 12, 1912 (see pg. 26) and Yuan was elected President of the Republic of China two days later replacing Sun Yat-Sen.

Yuan moved the capital to **Beijing** soon after his appointment and the country prepared to hold its first national elections. After the revolution, the

Revolutionary Alliance along with several other revolutionary groups merged into the mainstream political party, the **Nationalist Party** or **Kuomintang** (**KMT**), which won the majority of the seats in the new National Assembly elected in early 1913.

The Kuomintang flag: a twelve ray white sun on a blue background.

YUAN SHIKAI (r. 1912-1916)

The republican experiment began to fall apart soon after its inception when President Yuan Shikai jockeyed for more power. President Yuan increasingly took control of the government by appointing supporters to governmental posts, ignoring the parliament (e.g. accepting foreign loans without consulting the legislature) and cracking down on the Kuomintang. Just one month after the elections, the Kuomintang parliamentary leader, **Song Jiaoren**, was assassinated generating wide speculation that Yuan Shikai was responsible.

To curb Yuan Shikai's dictatorial ambitions, in July 1913 Sun Yat-Sen and members of the Kuomintang attempted to stage a **second revolution** against Yuan (who still had the army behind him). The second revolution failed miserably and prompted Yuan to ban the KMT and then dismiss the parliament all together. For the next two years, Yuan revised the constitution to expand his term (to ten years with no term limit) and to broaden his powers (e.g. allowing him to declare war and to sign treaties without parliamentary approval). In 1915, Yuan began to pave the way for even greater ambitions by appeasing the Japanese. In May, Yuan Shikai signed the controversial **Twenty-one Demands** which expanded Japan's sphere of influence in southern Manchuria and Inner Mongolia. A few months later, Yuan proclaimed himself "Emperor" igniting local rebellions and provincial declarations of independence. Faced with extreme hostility, he finally abandoned his monarchical ambitions just a few months before his death in June 1916.

WARLORD PERIOD (1916-1928)
As long as the military remained loyal to their former commander, Yuan Shikai was able to maintain a degree of centralized authority. Without their leader, though, the army disintegrated into small personal militias commanded by local competing warlords.

The fragmentation of China crippled the country politically, economically and socially. Trade and industry declined due to corruption and transportation problems. The opium business was revived to generate income for local leaders. The people were burdened with heavy taxes and continuous warfare. And China as a country was represented internationally by a string of warlords who had taken power in Beijing (called the "**Beiyang Government**" after the Beiyang Army).

One of those warlords, **Premier Duan Qirui**, saw his best interests served by China's involvement in **World War I**.

WORLD WAR I

Initially China had declared itself neutral in the war that pitted the **Allied Entente Powers** (the British Empire, France, the Russian Empire, Japan and the United States) against the **Central Powers** of Germany, Austria-Hungary, the Ottoman Empire and Bulgaria.

But in 1917, hoping to receive money from the Japanese (no doubt to bolster his own militia) then-Premier **Qirui** (r. 1916-1920) declared war on Germany and committed tens of thousand of Chinese soldiers to fight on behalf of the Allied Entente Powers. In return for their contribution, the Chinese hoped to recover the regions in **Shangdong Province** that had been occupied by Germany.

However, when the terms of peace were hammered out in **Versailles**, the victorious Entente Powers instead handed the **Shandong** province over to the Japanese causing a national uproar.

MAY FOURTH MOVEMENT

On May 4, 1919, thousands of students in Beijing staged a mass demonstration to protest the betrayal of the **Versailles Treaty** and sought punishment for the traitorous Chinese diplomats who had attended the conference. They were joined the next day by students in other parts of China as well as workers, businessmen and other alienated Chinese citizens.

The demonstrators were somewhat successful. Some politicians were dismissed and the government refused to sign the Versailles Treaty (although Japan kept control of Shangdong) but the uprising led to something even greater, the development of a **New Culture Movement**.

The age of emperors had collapsed and with it, the trust in Confucianism and ancient tradition. The republican government had been a failure and the current regimes were too corrupt and fragmented to be effective. Moreover, the Chinese believed the Americans (who otherwise would have been in a good position to influence China) were hypocrites – promoting the right of nations to decide how they would be governed without the interference of another country ("self-determination" as outlined in **Woodrow Wilson's Fourteen Points** listed in a speech he gave to the American Congress in 1918) while they were depriving China of exactly this right.

Alternatively, many intellectuals turned to Russia for guidance by embracing the theories of **Karl Marx** and studying the 1917 Soviet **Bolshevik Revolution.**

CHINESE COMMUNIST PARTY (CCP)
With the help of the Soviet Union's **International Communist Organization** or "**Comintern,**" Chinese communists held their first meeting in Shanghai in July 1921. This was an association founded by **Vladimir Lenin** in 1919 with the aim of overthrowing the bourgeoisie (see box pg. 63) worldwide and creating an international Soviet Republic. The new **Chinese Communist Party (CCP)** was still small compared to Sun Yat-Sen's Kuomintang, but under the leadership of a then-minor delegate, **Mao Zedong,** the CCP would eventually become the most powerful force in China.

REEMERGENCE OF THE KUOMINTANG
In 1914 after Yuan Shikai dismissed the parliament, Sun Yat-Sen took up residence in Japan where he developed the new "**Chinese Kuomintang.**" In 1917, he returned to China and set up a rival government in Guangzhou.

After the 1919 **May Fourth Movement,** Sun Yat-Sen approached Western nations for aid to reorganize the KMT. When the Western countries rejected him, he turned to Soviet leaders – who were themselves looking for allies in Asia. The Soviets offered to help the KMT develop a military force (the **National Revolutionary Army [NRA]**), and train prominent communist party members in Moscow, among them, KMT lieutenant **Chiang Kai-Shek.** But as a provision for their assistance, the KMT had to collaborate with the new Chinese Communist Party. Together as the **United Front,** the Soviets, KMT and Chinese Communists prepared to embark on a **Northern Expedition** from the KMT stronghold in Guangdong Province to defeat the warlords and the Beiyang government in Beijing.

DEATH OF SUN YAT-SEN (1925)
Not all members of the Kuomintang were as accepting of the collaboration between the KMT and the Communist Party as was Sun Yat-Sen. After Sun's death in 1925, a power struggle ensued between the rightists, led by **Chiang Kai-Shek,** who rejected the CCP, and those who favored cooperating with the CCP, led by **Wang Jingwei,** Sun's successor as Chairman of the KMT.

Chiang Kai-Shek, who wielded great influence as commander of the **National Revolutionary Army**, eventually supplanted Wang as head of the KMT, months before launching the **Northern Expedition** on July 27, 1926.

NORTHERN EXPEDITION (1926)
Because of the Soviet aid, the National Revolutionary Army was better armed, organized and trained than the warlord militias and was well received by China's peasants and workers who were exhausted by continuous warfare

and exploitation. Within nine months, half of China had been conquered and Chiang Kai-Shek's prestige soared.

The swift victories reinforced Chiang's Kai-Shek's position as the paramount leader of the **United Front**. But he became increasingly distrustful of the Communists who, he feared were preparing to seize the government.

SHANGHAI MASSACRE (April 12 Incident)
When the National Revolutionary Army reached Shanghai on April 12, 1927 Chiang Kai-Shek issued a secret order to expel all the Communists from the KMT. Thousands of Communists were arrested and executed in the following days including Chinese Communist Party co-founder **Li Dazhao**. Those who escaped persecution (among them future Communist leader **Mao Zedong**) fled to rural regions in China.

The Kuomintang established its capital in **Nanjing** and, after the purge (the ridding of a political party of disloyal members), went on to defeat the rest of China's warlords. In June 1928 the KMT captured the warlords' capital of **Beijing** and was henceforth recognized internationally as China's sole legitimate government.

NANJING DECADE (1927-1937)
Under the rule of **Generalissimo[43] Chiang Kai-Shek**, the Nanjing government endeavored to modernize the country and reverse some of the **unequal treaties** that had been made with Western powers and Japan.

Tens of thousands of miles of new railroads and highways were constructed and, with the founding of the **China Aviation Company** in 1930, regular flights transported people between major cities in China. New hospitals were opened and the government launched an extensive educational program opening many universities and teachers-training institutes. In 1935 the government decreed that silver would be nationalized and ordered all people who were in possession of bullion (gold and silver) to exchange their supplies for paper currency. The money earned by the state during the conversion helped fund modest industrialization.

In 1934, Chiang Kai-Shek and his wife **Soong Mayling** (also known as "**Madame Chiang Kai-Shek**"), who was the sister of Sun Yat-Sen's widow, initiated the **New Life Movement**, a campaign to revive the national spirit by restoring Confucian morals and principles. Honor, courtesy and filial duty were promoted as well as personal hygiene, etiquette and other habits.

---

[43] In 1928 Chiang Kai-Shek (known in China as Jiang Jieshe) adopted the military title of Generalissimo of all Chinese Forces.

The KMT ruled autocratically since no competing parties were permitted to function. But the KMT only governed about a third of the nation. The rest of the country was ruled by local warlords who periodically rebelled against the government. But the greatest enemies to the state, according to the Generalissimo, were the Communists who had a program, strong and capable leadership and popular support.

Communists to Countryside

After the KMT purge in April 1927 the Communists were forced to go underground or relocate to the countryside where they established a strong support base. The Communists were particularly welcomed in areas of southern China where there were large disparities between the lifestyles of the rich and the poor. The concepts of social equality, land distribution and a collective lifestyle greatly appealed to impoverished workers and peasants who had long been exploited by landlords.

But the Communists were under constant threat from Chiang Kai-Shek who launched a series of military campaigns in the 1930s, encircling and then annihilating Communist bases.

LONG MARCH (Oct. 1934-Oct. 1935)

When the constrictions became too oppressive, rather than risk annihilation, a group of 100,000 Communists led by **Mao Zedong** set out on a "**long march**" from their base in the Jiangxi Province in southeast China to Yan'an, a city in the north-central province of Shaanxi. Less than a fifth of the party survived the 6,000 mile trek through swamps and rivers and across snow-covered mountains –

but the survivors went on to create a model Communist community in their new home and would be portrayed as the party's heroic core.

JAPANESE INVASION (1931-1945)

While the Communists and Nationalists (KMT) engaged in a civil war, the Japanese, in search of raw materials and land for its growing population,[44] were descending into China from the northeast.

In September 1931, the Japanese seized the city of **Mukden**. Within a year,

---

[44] Only 20% of Japan's land is arable and the country lacks raw materials. Japan's population had also grown tremendously by the 1930s. By taking over Korea (in 1910) and then the resource-rich Manchuria, the Japanese hoped they could become self-sufficient while acquiring "living space" for its surplus population.

they had occupied all of
Manchuria, renamed it
Manchukuo and installed the
former Qing Emperor, **Puyi,**
as the head of state of a pup-
pet-government.

In order to save resources,
ammunition and fighting
power for defeating the
Communists, Chiang Kai-
Shek had ordered the
Kuomintang forces not to
resist the Japanese until the
"domestic enemies" (the
Communists) had been defeated. But the policy of non-resistance aroused
anger among the people and the military while the Japanese were making
their way through Inner Mongolia and Hebei with little opposition.

1936 XI'AN INCIDENT

While Chiang Kai-Shek was in Xi'an trying to urge his military to more
forcefully subdue the Communists, his troops mutinied and took him cap-
tive. After some negotiations, the soldiers agreed to release Chiang Kai-Shek
as long as he agreed to collaborate with the Communists. The Communists
and Nationalist Kuomintang temporarily put their differences aside to fight
the invading foreign enemy – the Japanese.

SECOND SINO-JAPANESE WAR (1937-1945)

The war formally started on July 7, 1937 when shots were fired at the **Marco
Polo Bridge** near Beijing. Within a few days, the Japanese began a full-scale
invasion capturing Beijing in July and working their way to Shanghai where
they committed terrible atrocities. From the "gateway to Nanjing (then
called 'Nanking')," the Japanese continued west to the Kuomintang capital
massacring hundreds of thousands of Chinese civilians and brutally raping
the women. Reports of the atrocities[45] in the course of the **Rape of Nanking**
in December 1937 reached the West through accounts of foreigners living in
that city. The reports were instrumental in turning American public opinion
against Japan during World War II.[46]

---

[45] The Japanese and Chinese have long disagreed about the degree and extent of the atrocities
committed by the Japanese in Nanjing and other Chinese cities during the Second Sino-
Japanese war.

[46] The Japanese attack on civilians in Shanghai and Nanjing was the subject of a 1944 Frank
Capra film: "The Battle of China." The film was one in a series of seven propaganda films
collectively called "Why We Fight" commissioned by the U.S. to show Americans why the
U.S. entered World War II. The Nanjing massacre was also the subject of a 2007 documen-
tary called "Nanking" starring Woody Harrelson.

After the Nanjing massacre, the KMT, along with millions of Chinese civilians, fled thousands of miles inland to **Chungking** (today Chongqing) in the Sichuan Province while Chiang Kai-Shek and his wife appealed to the world for support.

In the north, the Communists resorted to guerrilla warfare to fight the Japanese while drawing upon the nationalistic enthusiasm to promote their own socialist agenda. Administrative reforms were enacted in the villages under Communist influence, schools were established, rents were lowered, cooperatives were organized and land and tax-reforms favoring the peasants were adopted. They also empowered women by incorporating them as equal and important players in the fight against Japan and in preparation for the Communist Revolution.[47]

Almost from the beginning of their alliance, the Communists and Nationalists continued to clash. The Communists tried to consolidate their power base while they fought the external enemy and the Nationalists tried to neutralize growing Communist influence. By 1938 the Communist-KMT union was effectively falling apart.

AMERICANS AND WORLD WAR II
In September 1939, Germany under the command of **Adolf Hitler** invaded Poland sparking European engagement in the **Second World War** between the **Axis** powers of Nazi Germany, Italy and Japan against the **Allies**, the United Kingdom, the Soviet Union and, entering after the Japanese bombed Pearl Harbor, Hawaii, on December 7, 1941, the United States.

One of the main reasons the Americans entered the war was the fear that Japan was planning to dominate the world by first conquering China then establishing bases in the Pacific and finally conquering the United States as laid out in the **Tanaka Memorial**[48] (a document now regarded as a forgery).

The Chinese attempted to hold off the Japanese by keeping them engaged in skirmishes and ambushing their forces. But the war took a turn in mid-1941 when the Americans deployed volunteer air units called the **Flying Tigers** and cut-off Japan's oil supply. The embargo prompted the Japanese to invade the Dutch East Indies in search of natural resources and to bomb **Pearl Harbor** in the U.S. to prevent the Americans from deploying their navy to stop them. The Japanese finally surrendered in August 1945 after the U.S. dropped atomic bombs on the Japanese cities of Hiroshima and Nagasaki in retaliation – killing more than 100,000 Japanese civilians.

---

[47] In 1950 the Communists enacted the first Marriage Law granting women the privilege of divorce. In 1953, women were given the right to vote. They were also permitted the same rights as men to possess or inherit property.

[48] The Tanaka Memorial is mentioned in Frank Capra's film "Battle of China" and is the theme of the James Cagney 1945 film "Blood on the Sun."

By war's end, twenty million Chinese had died at the hands of the Japanese and the economy was in shambles. The end of the war also reignited the civil war in China – beginning with the conflict over who would receive the surrendering Japanese troops in northern China.

Civil War Reignited

The Western powers recognized Chiang Kai-Shek as China's legitimate leader and directed all aid to the Kuomintang (even airlifting KMT troops to the north and forcing the Japanese to surrender only to the KMT Nationalists). But Chiang

Kai Shek's government had become corrupt, its military had been decimated by war and the country was struggling due to uncontrolled government spending and rampant inflation.

The Communists, by contrast, were highly regarded locally for their efforts fighting the Japanese in northern China and commanded the support of the vast population of poorer workers and peasants, and even dispirited former KMT troops – many of whom joined the Chinese Communist Party's "People's Liberation Army."[49]

With Soviet backing, the PLA attacked the KMT forces from bases in Manchuria, now abandoned by the Japanese. By late 1949, the Communists had made their way down to the northern bank of the Yangtze River forcing the KMT to retreat to the island of **Taiwan**. From their first days in exile, the KMT, still recognized by the West as China's government, vowed to recover their rule over mainland China. (See pg. 102)

On **October 1, 1949**, from Tiananmen Square, the Chinese Communist Party's leader **Mao Zedong**, hero of the Long March, formally declared the establishment of the **People's Republic of China**.

PEOPLE'S REPUBLIC OF CHINA

Within two years after the founding of the PRC, nearly all the territory that had been ruled by the Qing Emperors was recovered and China was again united.

But when it came to enacting reforms there were two schools of thought. Moderates, like Politburo Member **Liu Shaoqi** believed that the **Communist Revolution** ought to begin as philosopher **Karl Marx** had theorized, through the traditional development of industry. (See pg. 63)

---

[49] The Peoples Liberation Army (PLA) was an offshoot of the Red Army created in 1927.

The more powerful radicals led by CCP Chairman **Mao Zedong**, though, maintained that in order to finance industrialization, the government would have to take control of agriculture. Towards that end, the new government enacted the 1950 **Agrarian Law** which confiscated land and property owned by landlords and redistributed it to the peasants. Millions of landlords were publicly ridiculed as "bureaucratic capitalists" and forced to attend "re-education" classes or endure vigilante justice taken by angry, murderous peasants. A few years after the Agrarian Law had been enacted, rural farmers were gathered into agricultural cooperatives modeled on Soviet-style **collective farms**.

The new communist leaders enacted laws giving women equality in marriage and granting them divorce rights. They denounced all forms of religion and mysticism and set up programs to educate the rural population and eradicate opium addiction. In 1956, they distributed internal passports to all Chinese citizens in order to limit movement within the country.

FIRST GENERATION OF POLITICAL LEADERS
Years: 1949-1976
Headed By: Mao Zedong
Other Members: Zhou Enlai, Liu Shaoqi, Peng Dehuai, Lin Biao and the Gang of Four
Ideologies: Marxism and Mao Zedong Thought

SOVIET UNION

Just two months after the declaration of the Chinese People's Republic, Mao Zedong traveled to the Soviet Union to get recognition for the new Communist regime and to ask for aid. After three months in Moscow, Chairman Mao and the General Secretary of the Communist Party of the Soviet Union, **Joseph Stalin**, signed the **Sino-Soviet Treaty of Friendship, Alliance and Mutual Assistance.** The Russians agreed to send technical advisers and aid to China in exchange for the right to keep a naval base in the Liaodong Peninsula among other privileges.

Communist China's relationship with the "capitalistic and bourgeois" West, by contrast, was frosty as long as the Americans and Europeans continued to side with Chiang Kai-Shek and the Taiwan-based KMT (which the West still considered China's legitimate government).

KOREAN WAR (1950)

After the surrender of Japan at the end of World War II in 1945, the **Korean Peninsula** (which had been under Japanese control since 1910) was divided at the 38th parallel and occupied by Russia in the north and the U.S. in the south. Both countries had helped install Korean-led governments that reflected compatible political ideologies. In the north, the Soviets supported the rise of Korean socialist General Secretary **Kim Il-Sung**. In the south, the Americans backed anti-communist strongman **Syngman Rhee**. Both leaders hoped to reunify Korea under their control but it was the North Koreans who made the first aggressive attempt to overtake their southern nemesis on June 25, 1950.

The United Nations entered the conflict in October 1950 forcing the North Koreans to retreat back behind the 38th parallel line that separated the Koreas. The UN entry into the war greatly alarmed the Chinese who feared that if the Americans occupied all of Korea, they would eventually declare war on China. In desperation, the Chinese backed the North Koreans and asked the Soviets for help.

After three years of fighting, the war ended in 1953 in a stalemate with the 38th parallel being deemed a **demilitarized zone** (DMZ).

However, China's performance in the Korean War demonstrated the power of China's military to the world and motivated Mao to begin developing an **atomic bomb** (which was completed in 1964). China's involvement also prompted the Americans and their allies to institute an economic embargo to isolate China from the non-Communist world.

China's relationship with the Soviet Union was also fading after the death of **Joseph Stalin** and due to a general feeling that the Soviets didn't offer the Chinese enough aid in the Korean War. Mao was particularly critical of the revisionist policies of Stalin's successor, First Secretary **Nikita Khrushchev** (who, in 1956, announced a **de-Stalinization** policy) and aimed to lead China rapidly towards a socialist utopia in a uniquely Asian way.

ONE HUNDRED FLOWERS CAMPAIGN (1956)

In order to jump-start reform and revive the revolutionary spirit, Mao Zedong initiated a period of free speech encouraging intellectuals to openly voice their complaints. Hundreds of thousands of students, scholars, artists and officials took Mao seriously when he proclaimed "let a hundred flowers bloom and a hundred schools of thought contend," and they criticized not only abuses by party officials but the Chinese Communist Party itself and its policies.

But almost as suddenly as the policy of open criticism had been enacted, the CCP reversed it. Those who had spoken out now found themselves the victims of an anti-rightist campaign leading many historians to theorize that the whole exercise was just a trap intended to weed out anyone critical of the regime. Thousands of people were imprisoned as a result and half a million "rightist" intellectuals were sent to work in the countryside. Intellectuals and specialists were afraid to speak out from that point on resulting in dire consequences.

GREAT LEAP FORWARD (1958-1962)

Mao Zedong believed a socialist Utopia could only be achieved if the country aggressively and concurrently developed agriculture and industry. The goal of the "**Great Leap Forward**" was to increase China's steel production beyond that of the United Kingdom and to double agricultural production through central planning and collective labor.

In 1958, the ruling Political Bureau of the Chinese Communist Party (or **Politburo**) organized peasants into 24,000 self-sufficient **communes** each made up of 5,000 households. All work was divided equally. Meals were shared and salaries were replaced by work points. Those who didn't tend the fields worked in steel production manning the small "**backyard**" **steel furnaces** that each neighborhood was encouraged to set up.

Although there were some achievements, most of the projects had disastrous outcomes. Because of the high quotas and overly ambitious promises of the commune leaders, more and more effort was put into steel production at the expense of agriculture. The steel that was produced, moreover, was impure and unusable since the inexperienced but enthusiastic peasants dropped pots, pans, rakes, irons and other sundry household items into the furnaces.

Agricultural yield was actually smaller than in previous years in many places due to experimental but destructive agricultural methods and the loss of labor (since many men were diverted away from the fields to work on steel production). Adding to the problem, in the spirit of the Revolution, local leaders frequently exaggerated the yield of the fields. Since quotas were based on the size of the harvest, the collective farms were obliged to send most of their crops to the cities in fulfillment of inflated quotas leaving little for the peasants. The situation worsened due to droughts, floods and swarms of locusts. By 1961, tens of millions of people had reportedly died from starvation.

LUSHAN CONFERENCE (1959)

The failures of the Great Leap Forward were openly addressed at the 1959 party conference at Lushan in the Jiangxi Province. Although Mao wasn't held completely responsible for the failures, he agreed to step down as Chairman of the People's Republic of China in order "to concentrate on ideological work." More moderate Politburo member **Liu Shaoqi** took his place with **Deng Xiaoping** serving as the CCP's General Secretary.

Many of the damaging Great Leap policies were reversed including ceasing the export of grain (which Mao had continued despite shortages in order to maintain China's international reputation), closing collective farms and ending local steel production. As China's economy recovered, Liu Shaoqi and Deng Xiaoping became more popular causing Mao to fear that he would be overshadowed.

While the moderates, Liu Shaoqi and Deng Xiaoping, were occupied with day-to-day management of the country, Mao was planning his comeback.

CULT OF PERSONALITY AND THE "LITTLE RED BOOK"

From the sidelines, Mao was developing a vast following by cultivating a **Cult of Personality** that would reach mythical proportions by the late 1960s. With the help of Defense Minister **Lin Biao**, Mao Zedong held sway over the **People's Liberation Army** and took great measures to build it into a model communist institution. Soldiers were encouraged to follow Mao's instructions and study his ideology as outlined in the **"Little Red Book,"** a collection of quotations from Mao's speeches and publications compiled by Lin Biao in 1964. Within a few years millions of students and other revolutionaries owned copies of the pocket-sized book and it became required practice to study Mao's quotations in schools and at the workplace.

SINO-SOVIET RELATIONS

After the establishment of the People's Republic of China (PRC) in 1949 the Chinese had looked to the Soviet Union for guidance and aid. But the relationship broke down after the death of **Joseph Stalin**. In 1959, the Soviets under Stalin's successor, **Nikita Khrushchev,** held a summit meeting with American President **Dwight D. Eisenhower**. A year later they withdrew their advisers and aid from China and, in 1962, refused to back the Chinese in skirmishes against India. By the time the Soviets signed a nuclear test-ban treaty with the United States and Great Britain in 1963, the Chinese were convinced that they needed to be self-sufficient militarily. The next year, China successfully exploded its first atomic bomb.

In Mao's opinion, the Soviets were falling down a slippery slope away from the Marxist-Leninist ideals of worldwide communism toward conciliation with the capitalists in the West. In order to prevent China from following suit Mao insisted that China needed to step-up the revolutionary struggle politically and culturally. A **"cultural revolution,"** he reasoned, would rid the country of all institutions and people who stood in the way of progress. It would also undermine Mao's moderate leaning rivals.

GREAT PROLETARIAN CULTURAL REVOLUTION (1966)

The Cultural Revolution began to take off in the spring of 1966 when a young philosophy teacher put up a **"big-character poster"** (*dazibao*) denouncing the Beijing University authorities as "reactionaries." With Mao's encouragement, students throughout China put up their own posters, held mass meetings and began to organize rebellions. With "Little Red Book" in hand, this new cadre of urban youth organized as **"Red Guards"** was mobilized by Mao and the Central Committee to attack everything that represented the **Four**

Olds: "Old Customs, Old Culture, Old Habits and Old Ideas" and were urged to struggle against those persons in authority who were taking the "capitalist road."

Millions of Red Guards from around the country answered the call, destroying religious institutions and symbols of China's imperialistic past and taunting, beating or killing anyone who could be labeled a reactionary, counterrevolutionary or moderate "**capitalist roader**." Landlords, doctors, professors and other "exploitative" authority figures were forced to parade through the streets wearing placards identifying their "crimes" against the revolution while the police, who were ordered not to interfere, looked on.

In the summer of 1967, the Cultural Revolution landed on the government's doorstep when tens of thousands of Red Guards forced the party's "greatest capitalist roader," Chairman **Liu Shaoqi**, to come out and face public humiliation. After power passed to Defense Minister **Lin Biao** and Mao Zedong's wife, **Jiang Qing**, Liu Shaoqi was expelled from the party and put under house arrest. He died in November 1969 after being denied medical care.

In April 1969, at the Ninth Party Congress, Mao Zedong announced that the Great Proletarian Cultural Revolution had been successful. Mao was reinstated as the country's leader with Lin Biao named Mao's successor and second-in-command.

In order to prevent the reemergence of anarchy and terror at the hands of the Red Guards, Mao sent millions of young urban intellectuals to the countryside where they would cause less disruption and "learn from the peasants." They remained there for the next decade.

LIN BIAO

After returning to power, Mao Zedong continued to expel government officials who only "appeared" to uphold the party line but who he felt were in fact disloyal. Among the victims was Mao's closest ally **Lin Biao** who was accused of secretly planning to oust Mao and take power himself. Lin Biao fled the country in fear in 1971 with his wife and son but before his plane landed in the Soviet Union, the aircraft mysteriously ran out of gas and crashed.

The purging and death of Lin Biao, once Mao's greatest ally, was disconcerting to many revolutionaries who began to conclude that they had been used as pawns in a political game. Political insecurity also led to corruption as officials learned to rely on personal relationships and influence to maintain their positions rather than efficiency and hard work.

ZHOU ENLAI vs. THE GANG OF FOUR

Power in China's government in the late 1960s and 1970s swung between the pragmatists led by **Zhou Enlai**, China's Premier of the State Council, and the radicals guided by Mao Zedong's wife, **Jiang Qing**, and her supporters, collectively called the **Gang of Four**.

Zhou Enlai had a long history as a revolutionary beginning with his participation in the May Fourth Movement in 1919 which landed him in prison. After he was released from jail, Zhou went to Europe where he became an activist in the expatriate Chinese Communist movement. Upon his return to China, Zhou took part in the Long March and, in 1936, helped persuade Chiang Kai-Shek to join in an alliance with the Communists against the Japanese. When the People's Republic of China was established in 1949, Zhou served as the PRC's first premier and Minister of Foreign Affairs. During the Cultural Revolution, he was responsible for curbing some of the worst excesses and saving some historical sites (including the Forbidden City).

Within China, Zhou Enlai was adored by the people because of his modesty, charm and intelligence. In the West, he was regarded as the diplomat who helped bridge relations between the PRC and the U.S.

PING-PONG DIPLOMACY

By the late 1960s relations between the PRC and the Soviet Union had deteriorated to the brink of war. The Chinese government was particularly concerned by the Soviets' adoption of the **Brezhnev Doctrine** which stated that the Soviets had the right to intervene in a country's affairs if they perceived a threat to the common interests of socialist countries.

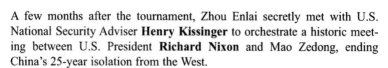

While the Soviets were building up troops on the Chinese-Soviet border, Zhou Enlai was advocating peaceful relations with the West, beginning with the extension of an invitation to the U.S. table tennis team to compete in China in April 1971 (a strategy that would later be known as "**ping-pong diplomacy**").[50]

A few months after the tournament, Zhou Enlai secretly met with U.S. National Security Adviser **Henry Kissinger** to orchestrate a historic meeting between U.S. President **Richard Nixon** and Mao Zedong, ending China's 25-year isolation from the West.

---

[50] The thaw in relations between China and the U.S. began when American ping-pong player Glenn Cowan missed his bus after practice during the World Table Tennis Championship in Japan in 1971. A member of the Chinese team that was also competing in Japan, invited him to ride on the Chinese bus back to his hotel 15 minutes away. The news about the brief but friendly interaction between citizens from enemy countries reached Mao Zedong who invited the American team to participate in a a demonstration game in China a few days later. The Chinese ping-pong player was invited to the U.S. shortly thereafter.

The meetings concluded with the signing of the **Shanghai Communique** on February 27, 1972 which pledged to normalize relations between the two countries and promised that neither would seek hegemony in the region. In regards to Taiwan, the U.S. agreed not to support Taiwan's independence movement – but would not suppress it either. (See pg. 102)

FOUR MODERNIZATIONS
Along with improving diplomatic relations between China, the West and other countries, Zhou Enlai promoted economic growth through a plan he coined the **"four modernizations"**: developing agriculture; industry; science and technology, and defense.

In order to aid in China's financial and political recovery, Zhou also brought back a number of people who had been purged during the Cultural Revolution including his good friend **Deng Xiaoping**.

GANG OF FOUR
On the other side of the political spectrum from Zhou Enlai and Deng Xiaoping were the radicals who favored the continuation of the Cultural Revolution. They advocated focusing on class struggle and egalitarianism and limiting relations with other countries. Mao's wife, **Jiang Qing** and her cohorts, known as the **Gang of Four,** also attacked Zhou Enlai accusing him of undoing progress by rehabilitating politicians who had been deemed "enemies of the state" and leading the country towards capitalism.

Mao Zedong tried to mediate between the moderate reformers, Zhou Enlai and Deng Xiaoping, and the Gang of Four radicals, but his health was declining.

In 1972, Mao suffered a severe stroke. Two years later, Zhou Enlai was hospitalized with incurable bladder cancer.

DEATH OF ZHOU ENLAI
When Zhou Enlai learned that he had a fatal illness, he began grooming **Deng Xiaoping** to succeed him. To the dismay of Jiang Qing and her followers, Deng Xiaoping assumed increasingly greater powers between 1974 and 1975 pushing forward Zhou Enlai's **"four modernizations"** and continuing to rehabilitate victims of the Cultural Revolution. When Zhou Enlai died on January 8, 1976, it was Deng Xiaoping who delivered his eulogy.

On April 4th during the **Qingming** festival, a traditional day when the Chinese grieve over departed loved ones, Zhou's death was deeply mourned by the people and widely commemorated. Hundreds of thousands of people gathered in **Tiananmen Square** to pay homage to the popular leader. Thousands also laid wreaths on the monument of the People's Heroes in the center of the Square. But along with poems dedicated to Zhou Enlai, some of the wreaths contained messages supporting Deng Xiaoping and denouncing Jiang Qing and the Gang of Four.

In response, the government removed all of the wreaths which enraged the grieving public and sparked a spontaneous uprising. Hundreds of people died when the government violently suppressed the riot.

The radicals took the opportunity to advance their positions by convincing Mao Zedong that Deng Xiaoping was responsible for the riot and for reversing the Cultural Revolution. Two days later, Deng Xiaoping was removed from power and replaced by **Hua Guofeng**, a relatively unknown politician who advocated strict adherence to Maoist orthodoxy, a plan he named the "**two whatevers**": "*Whatever* policies Chairman Mao set we will continue to uphold. *Whatever* orders Chairman Mao gave, we will continue to follow."

Hua Guofeng and his unpopular agenda didn't last long – nor did the authority of the Gang of Four.

MAO ZEDONG'S DEATH

On September 9, 1976, Mao Zedong died of heart and lung ailments. Mao's death brought mixed emotions from the populace. On one hand, the people mourned the passing of the architect of the Chinese Revolution; on the other hand, they were eager to see the final political demise of Mao's wife, Jiang Qing, and the hated Gang of Four (whose careers were doomed without Mao's backing).

The Gang of Four was duly arrested a month after Mao's death and put on trial in 1981. Jiang Qing and the Gang were blamed for the horrors that took place during the Cultural Revolution and charged with attempting to seize power. They were held responsible for all the devastation that had taken place in the 10-year period as well as the persecution of more than 700,000 citizens and the deaths of more than 30,000 people.

For their crimes one of the radicals was given 20 years in prison, another life in prison, and Jiang Qing and Zhang Chunqiao, who did not admit guilt, were given the death penalty (later commuted to life in prison). Mao's wife reportedly committed suicide after she was released in 1991.

DENG XIAOPING

After Mao Zedong died, the Party reinstated former General Secretary **Deng Xiaoping**, who had recently been ousted and was at home atoning for "political mistakes." In July 1977, he was made Vice Premier of the State Council, Vice-Chairman of the Central Committee, Vice-Chairman of the Military Commission and Chief of Staff of the People's Liberation Army. Hua Guofeng kept his position as a member of the

Central Committee but was replaced as Premier by rehabilitated reformer and Deng ally, **Zhao Ziyang**, and replaced as Chairman of the Communist Party by **Hu Yaobang** in 1981.

Deng Xiaoping called on the Party and the people to observe **Four Cardinal Truths**: the principles of Communism, the total power of the Communist Party and the theories of Marxism-Leninism and Mao Zedong Thought. But he deviated from Hua Guofeng's "two whatevers" theory, which blindly gave credit to all of Mao's policies, by distinguishing between Maoist thought and the later errors in its application. Deng Xiaoping condemned class struggle (which had prevented many capable people from rising to power because of their status as landlords or intellectuals) and deemed the Cultural Revolution a mistake that had been fueled by the Gang of Four and **Lin Biao**. By allowing the public to criticize the excesses of the Cultural Revolution, Deng strengthened the position of those (like himself) who had been purged in that period.

> **SECOND GENERATION OF POLITICAL LEADERS**
>
> **Years:** 1976-1992
> **Headed By**: Deng Xiaoping
> **Other Members**: Hu Yaobang, Zhao Ziyang, Hua Guofeng
> **Ideology**: Deng Xiaoping Theory, Socialism with Chinese Characteristics, Four Modernizations

Deng Xiaoping adopted a new alternate concept of "**socialism with Chinese characteristics**" combining the essence of socialism with the management style used in capitalist countries.[51] The Communist Party would continue to maintain a monopoly on power but would allow a greater degree of free enterprise and rely on market forces (supply-and-demand) to make decisions. (See pg. 66)

He felt that the Chinese should be more flexible in their philosophical outlook and blaze their own economic trail, famously making his point by stating that "it doesn't matter whether a cat is black or white as long as it catches mice."

To that end, Deng Xiaoping concentrated on the "Four Modernizations" pioneered by Zhou Enlai, aimed at strengthening the country by modernizing agriculture, industry, science and technology and the military.

In the countryside (home to nearly 80% of China's population), communes were dissolved and peasants were encouraged to earn extra income by selling surplus produce on the open market. In the cities, Deng championed the position that some people and regions must get rich first and set an example to the rest of the country showing that hard work will result in rewards. The declaration resulted in a flurry of entrepreneurial activity that continues today.

Deng Xiaoping also advocated opening the country to foreign trade and diplomacy. In the 1980s the government created four **special economic zones (SEZs)**

---

[51] Deng Xiaoping's theories (also called "Dengism") have been required study in university classes in China since the 1980s. In 1997 Deng's theories were incorporated into China's Constitution.

(regions with especially liberal economic laws including the cities of Shenzhen, Shuhai, Shantou and Xiamen and the entire province of Hainan) and opened international access to 14 coastal cities to attract foreign investment.

To stimulate trade and enhance China's international image, Deng made several trips abroad meeting with Western leaders. After his visit with U.S. President **Jimmy Carter** in 1979, Carter severed diplomatic ties with **Taiwan** (the "Republic of China" or ROC) and established ties with communist China (the People's Republic of China or PRC).[52]

After meetings with British Prime Minister **Margaret Thatcher** in the early 1980s, Britain and China agreed to transfer sovereignty over **Hong Kong** to China in 1997.[53] Deng promised to preserve Hong Kong's capitalist economic system for fifty years through a system dubbed "**one-country, two-systems**" – allowing Hong Kong to maintain its own political system and capitalist financial institutions while the rest of China continued to practice socialism. The system was also applied to the colony of **Macau** which Portugal agreed to return to China in 1999.

Social and Economic Issues

The economic reforms and social liberties granted since 1978 greatly improved the lives of millions of Chinese. The freedom to travel permitted people to pursue jobs and educational prospects in other parts of the country giving them the opportunity to climb the social and economical ladder.

But the application of capitalist systems in parts of the country also created a huge wealth disparity separating affluent entrepreneurs and businessmen in China's coastal cities from poor peasants in the countryside. The reforms resulted in massive migration from the countryside to the cities by peasants seeking fortunes – or at least living wages – working as laborers in the cities.[54]

The changes also brought social ills long associated with capitalism: crime; prostitution; drugs; corruption and inflation. While many poor Chinese resented the rapid reforms which deprived them of social security and the safety of the commune system, others (for example students and intellectuals) complained that the reforms did not go far enough.

---

[52] In order to grant China formal diplomatic recognition on January 1, 1979, Carter first had to withdraw recognition from non-communist Taiwan and revoke the 1955 Mutual Defense Treaty with the Republic of China (Taiwan). However, the U.S. maintained quasi-diplomatic relations with Taiwan through the Taiwan Relations Act of 1979 and continued to supply Taiwan with arms to defend itself from mainland China (a source of continuous friction with the P.R.C.)

[53] Hong Kong was ceded to Britain in 1841 after the Opium Wars and was subject to full British sovereignty in 1898 through a 99-year lease (to expire in 1997).

[54] Before the 1980s travel within the country was severely limited and employment in regions outside one's hometown was forbidden without government permits.

TIANANMEN SQUARE INCIDENT (a.k.a. JUNE FOURTH INCIDENT)

Until the 21st century, China's government maintained a balancing act between Maoist socialism and Western capitalism reining in excesses on both ends of the spectrum.

One of the casualties of the government's drive for moderation was Party General Secretary **Hu Yaobang**, a dedicated reformer who pushed for greater political freedoms. Hu's popularity soared among student intellectuals when he refused to put down a wave of pro-democracy student protests in December 1986 and January 1987. But his liberal ideas[55] and sympathy for the demonstrators led to his dismissal by the Party's hard-liners a few months later. After two years in seclusion, Hu died of a heart attack in 1989 triggering one of the greatest demonstrations China had seen in decades.

Thousands of students gathered in squares around the country to mourn his death on April 15, days before the government, under public pressure, organized a state funeral. The gatherings continued after official mourning had ended drawing hundreds of thousands of students primarily to Tiananmen Square in Beijing. By April 21, teachers and students were boycotting classes and the assembly had turned into a protest. Students protested against authoritarianism and corruption and marched in favor of democracy and greater political freedoms. Urban workers, who joined the student protesters, demonstrated against inflation and other economic injustices.

The government, remembering the 1976 "Tiananmen Incident" which ousted the Gang of Four and brought the current regime to power, became increasingly alarmed by the chaos. On May 20, Martial Law was declared. When that didn't work, troops and tanks were deployed. Hundreds of thousands of students and other participants died in the ensuing violence and thousands more were thrown in jail while foreign news teams (who had traveled to China in order to cover the anticipated visit of Soviet leader Mikhail Gorbachev) caught much of the turmoil on film. The most compelling image of a lone unarmed man (dubbed by Time Magazine as the "unknown rebel") standing defiantly in the path of a massive tank immortalized the struggle of the demonstrators.

The containment of the 1989 Tiananmen Incident was followed by widespread government suppression and the reversal of some liberal reforms. Even today, the media is forbidden to discuss the protests and discussion about the uprising is considered a taboo subject within China.

---

55 Unlike other Party members, Hu Yaobang did not idealize Mao Zedong and was one of the first statesmen to abandon the "Mao suit" (loose trousers and a loose, high-collared, thigh-length jacket worn and popularized by Mao Zedong) in favor of a jacket and tie. Hu Yaobang even advocated the use of western utensils over chopsticks and suggested that Chinese diners should eat from individual plates in order to avoid the spread of disease (the Chinese customarily share dishes).

Internationally, Deng Xiaoping and the PRC government were widely condemned for the violent crackdown. As punishment, the U.S. under President **George H. Bush** and the European Community imposed an arms embargo (which was still in place in 2009). The images of civilians being attacked by government forces tainted China's image as a reforming nation and fueled arguments by Western critics, particularly the "**Blue Team**" an anti-China political lobby group in the U.S., that stated that China was a danger to world peace and U.S. interests.

DEATH OF DENG XIAOPING (1997)

A few days after the Tiananmen Square crackdown, Deng Xiaoping defended the decision to take drastic measures in order to combat what he called a "rebellious clique" that wanted to topple the Communist Party, topple the socialist system and establish a totally "Western-dependent bourgeois republic." In the same June 9, 1989 speech, he reaffirmed the merits of the "Four Cardinal Principles" and encouraged the country to continue moving towards reform and openness. To emphasize the point, Deng Xiaoping made one last tour of southern China in 1992 to campaign for continued economic development. Deng then retired from the political scene and died five years later.

JIANG ZEMIN

Taking Deng Xiaoping's place as "paramount leader" of China was **Jiang Zemin**, the former mayor of Shanghai who rose to prominence in 1989 because of his decisive action subduing rebels in Shanghai, China's largest city.[56] In 1989, Jiang Zemin became General Secretary of the Communist Party (taking the post from **Zhao Ziyang** who was forced to step down after being accused of being lenient towards the demonstrators) and assumed **Deng Xiaoping's** role as Chairman of the Central Military Commission. In 1993, Jiang became President of the PRC.

THIRD GENERATION OF POLITICAL LEADERS
Years: 1992-2003
Headed By: Jiang Zemin
Other Members: Li Peng, Zhu Rongji, Qiao Shi
Ideology: Three Represents

Jiang Zemin continued along Deng Xiaoping's path of economic reform by privatizing a number of state-owned enterprises and pouring money into China's **Special Economic Zones**.

Hong Kong

In July 1998, **Hong Kong** reverted to Chinese control as agreed upon (**Macau** followed in 1999). Living up to Deng Xiaoping's promise to the British, Jiang Zemin implemented a "**one country, two systems**" structure which allowed Hong Kong, operating as a "**special administrative region** (SAR)," to maintain

---

[56] After coming to power, Jiang Zemin promoted colleagues who had worked with him in Shanghai to prominent government posts. The group, pejoratively called the "Shanghai Clique," remained powerful players in the Party and the state, at times clashing with non-Clique members like future President Hu Jintao and Premier Wen Jiabao.

a capitalist economy while the rest of China continued to do business according to a "socialist" system. Under China's control, the port city of Hong Kong, one of four economically successful **Asian Tigers**,[57] served as an important export and distribution center for goods produced on the Chinese mainland.

Jiang Zemin and Foreign Affairs

To secure international trading partners, Jiang Zemin sought to end China's diplomatic isolation by traveling to seventy countries and visiting with dozens of world leaders.

The Chinese President wasn't shy about his interest in foreign cultures. On many occasions he attempted to communicate in the local language and in the U.S. he recited the Gettysburg Address and sang renditions of Elvis Presley songs. The outreach had some positive results.

After participating in a number of high-level exchanges with American officials (including President **Bill Clinton**), China reached a trade agreement with the U.S. that led to China's November 2001 entry into the **World Trade Organization (WTO)**.

> ### THREE GORGES DAM
>
> In 1994 construction began on the Three Gorges Dam on the Yangtze River, a controversial source of energy that would provide as much as 1/9th of the nation's electrical needs. Although the dam would be environmentally beneficial in a country that burns 50 million tons of polluting coal for energy, the project caused some of the most fertile land in China to become flooded leaving whole cities underwater and dislocating more than 1.2 million people – many, like the Ba people, who had lived and farmed on the land for generations.

World Trade Organization (WTO)

As a condition for joining the **WTO**, China had to lower tariffs and allow foreign firms to sell directly to Chinese consumers. In return, the quota on Chinese exports of textiles and clothing would be dropped and China would be internationally recognized as an equal trading partner. Premier **Zhu Rongji** (the mastermind behind China's economic reforms between 1998 and 2003) reasoned that the foreign competition would force managers in China's state-owned companies to become more efficient and innovative [58] stimulating China's economic development.

Olympics Bid

In July 2001, China won its long-sought bid to host the Summer Olympics in 2008. As with the WTO, the acceptance came with conditions. To get the bid, China had to promise to improve Human Rights, clean up the environment and allow foreign journalists to write freely about the games and China in gener-

---

[57] Along with South Korea, Taiwan, and Singapore, the export-driven economies of the economic "Tigers" of Asia were noted for their extremely rapid economic growth, high level of industrialization and skilled and educated workforce.

[58] Political bureaucracy (which guaranteed jobs for life) and bribery had stifled the Chinese people's incentive to work hard.

al.[59] In turn, China would have the opportunity to win back the world's respect after negative press received during the 1989 crackdown of Tiananmen Square demonstrators.

But despite the promises and expectations, China didn't make any significant political reforms. Centralized power was carefully guarded and the government kept a tight rein on dissident behavior.

Falun Gong (see pg. 78)

One of the primary targets of governmental attack was a movement based on the tenets of Buddhism, Daoism and Qigong breathing exercises called Falun Gong. Falun Gong's leaders claimed the movement had grown to 60 million followers since it was founded in 1992 – more than the number of members in the China's Communist Party – and large groups could be seen publicly practicing Falun Gong exercises around the country. Though the movement promoted non-violence and had no apparent political agenda, the sheer number of adherents greatly alarmed China's Central government.

The potential threat of Falun Gong loyalty hit the Chinese government in 1999 when ten thousand Falun Gong practitioners assembled peacefully outside China's seat of power in Zhongnanhai to protest police brutality.[60]

In response to the show of strength, Jiang Zemin's government declared the movement a "threat to social stability" and detained thousands of members (Falun Gong says dozens of adherent were tortured to death). From that point on, followers were prohibited from holding meetings, distribution of Falun Gong materials was outlawed and public *qigong* exercises were banned.

NATO Bombing

Around the same time, in the course of a military campaign against the Federal Republic of Yugoslavia, NATO forces bombed the Chinese Embassy in Belgrade killing three PRC citizens. NATO and the CIA said the accidental hit was due to reliance on outdated maps but the Chinese public believed that the attack had been deliberately orchestrated to intimidate China.[61] The popular outrage within

---

[59] The members of the International Olympics Committee (IOC) hoped that the bid would stimulate reform as it had in South Korea. After South Korea won its bid to host the 1988 Summer Olympics, more than 2000 political dissidents were released from jail including future President Kin Dae-jung. And due to public outrage after a brutally suppressed riot, the country enjoyed democratic elections for the first time in 1987.

[60] In April 1999 police had been called to disband a protest over an article published in the Tianjin College of Education Reader magazine criticizing Falun Gong.

[61] There was speculation that the intended targets were Serbian leader Slobodan Milosevic, who was expected to be in the Embassy at the time of the attack, or Serbian war criminal "Arkan" who showed up at the Embassy soon after the bombing. It was also speculated that the attack was meant for the Chinese Embassy in retribution for China's help broadcasting Serbian signals to the Yugoslavian army.

China conveniently redirected attention away from the Falun Gong demonstration and potentially incendiary 10th anniversary of the 1989 Tiananmen protests.

Criticisms

As mayor of Shanghai, Jiang Zemin had been dubbed the "flowerpot" by critics – more decoration than a man of action. Later, he was accused of being too conciliatory towards the U.S. and Russia and of being more concerned with building his own image than dealing with festering social problems.

Jiang Zemin was the first Chinese leader since Mao Zedong to manipulate the media to ensure that his achievements would be front page news and the daily top story on the air. Even his signature theory, the **Three Represents,** was criticized as a weak philosophy that was concocted to put him on the same level as Mao Zedong and Deng Xiaoping.[62] Proponents of the Three Represents theory (see box) say it effectively incorporated entrepreneurs and members of the capitalist business class into the party.

> **Jiang Zemin's THREE REPRESENTS**
>
> "The Communist Party of China representing the requirements of the development of China's advanced productive forces, the orienting of the development of China's advanced culture and the fundamental interest of the overwhelming majority of the Chinese people."

To his successor, Jiang Zemin left many of the problems that he had inherited: rampant government corruption, wealth gaps between urban and rural dwellers. a surge in crime rates, staggering unemployment and environmental concerns – all issues that had resulted from rapid economic growth.

HU JINTAO

In 2002, Jiang Zemin began handing over leadership of the party to **Hu Jintao**. Hu assumed the position of General Secretary of the Communist Party of China in 2002, President of the People's Republic of China in 2003 and Chairman of the Central Military Commission by 2004.

At the **Third Plenary Session of the 16th Central Committee** (the third full meeting of the 16th Central Committee [in session from 2002-2007] of China's Communist Party) in Beijing in October 2003, Hu Jintao made clear his intention to focus attention away from all-out economic growth towards easing social tensions in order to

---

62 The Three Represents Theory was written into China's constitution in 2003 joining the theories of Marx, Lenin, Mao Zedong and Deng Xiaoping.

63 In 2005, President Hu Jintao quoted Confucius saying "Harmony is something to be cherished." The reference to the 6th century B.C. philosopher was in line with the government's campaign to promote Confucian values of filial piety (important in a a nation with poor social security), respect for authority and just and moral rule – although not to the exclusion of Marxism.

build a "**Harmonious Socialist Society.**"[63] Among the promises made by Hu Jintao and Premier **Wen Jiabao** were pledges to improve rural education and farmers' incomes (the urban-rural income gap was three to one), to improve industrial safety (especially in the coal mines,[64]) to re-employ workers, and address environmental degradation.

Along with easing social and economic woes, the Chinese Central government planned to focus on preparations for its "coming-out party" at the 2008 Summer Olympics. In just five years, Beijing would be expected to accommodate more than 10,000 athletes and millions of foreign visitors.

In order to relieve congestion on the roads, seven new subway lines were added to Beijing's subway system. A new airport terminal, the largest in the world, was built and thousands of buses were added to the existing fleet. As opening day approached, stricter rules were enacted letting fewer and fewer vehicles travel through the city.

> **FOURTH GENERATION OF POLITICAL LEADERS**
>
> **Years:** 2003 - 2013
> **Headed By**: Hu Jintao
> **Other Members**:Wen Jiabao, Jia Qinglin, Zeng Qinghong
> **Ideologies**: Scientific Development Concept and Harmonious Society

More than $40 billion was spent on construction for the Olympics including the building of an impressive national stadium dubbed the "bird's nest" because of its unique nest-like grid formation. Fifty-nine training centers were constructed as well as an Olympic Village with forty two buildings, a restaurant, an entertainment center, a library, and exercise quarters. Even the population received behavioral instructions in order to make the Chinese appear more refined. Public spitting was discouraged and healthful living was encouraged. Beijing residents were also instructed to respect traffic rules and to practice standing in orderly lines.

Bird's Nest Stadium

Environmental Issues
Ten of the world's most polluted cities in the world are in China. Rapid and unabated industrialization has polluted nearly all of China's rivers depriving hundreds of millions of Chinese of clean water. The air in more than 75% of China's cities is considered polluted causing hundreds of thousands of premature deaths from respiratory problems (one of the leading causes of death in China). And the spewing toxic chemicals from coal-burning power plants are reportedly responsible for an increase of nearly 40% of birth defects in China as well as global climate changes.

---

[64] China mines more coal than any other country in the world but the industry remains one of the most dangerous in China. Though Chinese miners earn slightly more than peasants, they are 117 times more likely to be killed at work than American miners (thousands die every year) and must endure abominable working conditions.

According to Hu Jintao, an integral element in a "harmonious society" is man's relationship with nature, inspiring Hu and Premier Wen Jiabao to devote a great amount of resources to reversing environmentally damaging trends. In 2004, the government attempted to measure economic progress with consideration to ecological concerns by instituting a "**Green GDP**." The **Green Gross Domestic Product**[65] figured in the cost of water, air and solid waste pollution and the investment in environmental protection when calculating China's Gross Domestic Product. (In 2004, for example, the report revealed that environmental pollution had cost China $64 billion in economic losses, accounting for about 3% of China's GDP).[66] Hu Jintao's government also began protecting forests, holding national "no-car days" in dozens of cities and, in June 2008, they began banning ultra-thin plastic bags among other conservationist measures.

In order to ensure clean air during the Olympics, Beijing and surrounding factories were temporarily or permanently shut down. Tens of millions of trees were planted, sewage treatment was upgraded and energy efficient street lights were installed (in addition to strict measures to keep cars off the roads).

Despite China's attempts to improve its image abroad, the country could not escape international criticism.

Tainted Exports

In 2007, China's export market took a hit when U.S. company Mattel recalled 19 million Chinese-made items because they contained lead paint.[67] The same year, the National Highway Traffic Safety Administration recalled nearly 450,000 tires sold to the U.S. because they were susceptible to shredding on the roads. Pets across the United States were dying after consuming Chinese pet food that was laced with melamine (a compound used for plastic that had been added to the food to make protein content appear higher). In 2008, 53,000 Chinese children also fell ill after drinking melamine-tainted baby formula.

As intended, the world's eyes were increasingly directed towards China as the Olympics approached. But with the growing attention came greater degrees of scrutiny and condemnation of China's abhorrent human rights record, it's dealings with rogue countries like Darfur (see pg. 54) and its relationship with Tibet.

Human Rights Issues

Notwithstanding **Article 35** of China's constitution (see box on following page) and an amendment that states "the State respects and preserves human rights," China has maintained a long record of human rights violations that, according to the U.S. State Department and Human Rights Watch, was worse in 2008 in some areas than in previous years. Chinese citizens continue to see

---

65 The Green GDP was discontinued in 2007 when it was discovered just how high environmental damage had cost the nation.

66 The GDP evaluates economic output and income levels.

67 When ingested, lead can cause learning and physical disabilities in children.

their rights to privacy, free speech, assembly and movement limited. Chinese dissidents have been detained, tortured, exiled to labor camps or executed without proper adjudication. The Chinese government maintains strict control over the media, blocks internet access and, according to the human rights organization "Reporters Without Borders" China jails the greatest number of journalists, cyber-dissidents, Internet-users and freedom of expression campaigners in the world.

China's constitution also guarantees in Article 36 that citizens are to enjoy freedom of religious belief and "no state organ, public organization or

> **ARTICLE 35**
> **(Constitution of the P.R.C.)**
>
> "Citizens of the People's Republic of China enjoy freedom of speech, of the press, of assembly, of association, of procession and of demonstration."

individual... may discriminate against citizens who believe in, or do not believe in, any religion." But even Chinese who adhere to the five sanctioned faiths: Buddhism, Taoism, Islam, Catholicism and Protestantism have found their liberties trampled. Catholics who recognize the supremacy of the pope, for instance, risk being persecuted for their loyalty to a "foreign power." Members of churches that don't register with the state (called "house churches") are subject to government harassment and repression. The Chinese government has retained the right to expel Buddhist monks from monasteries and Islamic practices are tightly controlled (i.e. prayer in public areas outside the mosque is forbidden, sermons must not run longer than ½ hour, students and government workers must be allowed to eat during the holy fasting month of Ramadan etc.)

China's justification for its disregard for individual human rights lies in its desire to create a "harmonious society" that will serve the greatest number of people. In order to accomplish this, the Chinese leaders reason, they must take harsh measures to crackdown on "hostile forces" and "separatists."

Darfur

At the beginning of 2008, film director Steven Spielberg withdrew as artistic adviser for the 2008 Olympics citing China's continued support of Sudan as the reason. His sentiments echoed those of actress Mia Farrow, actor George Clooney and other celebrities who condemned China because it had not done enough to end the "human suffering" in Sudan's western Darfur region.[68]

China, which desperately needs oil and gas, buys two-thirds of Sudan's oil and, in return, sells the Sudanese government weapons. Reports have claimed that some Chinese imports (especially army trucks and fighter jets)

---

[68] Hundreds of thousands of people have been killed or raped in Darfur and more than two million have been forced from their homes by the local Arab Janjaweed fighters backed by the Sudanese government.

have been used in attacks against the villagers in Darfur.

Although China has begun to put pressure on Sudan's President Omar Hasan al-Bashir on the issue, the government argues that economic growth would more readily bring peace to the region than confrontation and sanctions.

Tibet

Even more inciting than China's support of Sudan in the West has been the government's treatment of Tibet. In 1951 China took control of Tibet claiming the region had been a part of the Chinese nation since the mid-13th century. Since then, the Chinese have destroyed important religious and cultural sites,[69] deprived the Tibetans of religious and political freedoms and forced the Tibetan Buddhists' leader, the Dalai Lama, to flee Tibet in 1959.[70]

In order to integrate the Autonomous Region of Tibet, the central government enticed ethnically Han Chinese to migrate to the high altitude region by offering financial incentives and promises of jobs and better housing. Han migration to Tibet accelerated dramatically in 2006 with the completion of the China-Tibet railway line (the highest train in the world) – resulting in Han Chinese populations outnumbering Tibetans in the capital, Lhasa, and fomenting local resentment as Han immigrants began monopolizing jobs and businesses. The cultural infusion and Chinese-funded modernization projects that followed altered the face of Tibet both physically and culturally (for example introducing karaoke bars and discotheques).

Unfortunately for the Chinese government, Tibetans angered over economic competition, the steady destruction of their traditions and with the general desire for independence, chose March of 2008 (the anniversary of a failed 1959 Tibetan uprising against Chinese rule), to make a stand. Just months before the Summer Olympics, media sources around the world aired images of Chinese security forces clashing with Buddhist monks and other Tibetans. (Within China, photos and videos of Tibetan rioters, arsonists and looters targeting Chinese-run banks, government offices and shops predominated). The conflict was a public relations nightmare for the Chinese government after months of work trying to enhance China's image.

"Great Sichuan Earthquake"

The international fury over the Tibetan conflict subsided somewhat when China was struck by another disaster. On the afternoon of May 12, 2008, China's Sichuan province was hit by an 8.0 magnitude earthquake that killed more than 1,700 people and left more than five million homeless. Images of

---

[69] China sees monasteries as hotbeds of dissent. To try to lessen the threat, the Chinese government has forced Tibetan monks to attend "re-education" sessions.

[70] After fleeing Tibet in 1959, Tenzin Gyatso, believed to be the 14th reincarnation of the Dalai Lama, set up and headed the Tibetan government-in-exile in Dharamsala, India.

battling monks and Chinese soldiers were quickly replaced internationally by those of sobbing parents and spontaneous compassionate community relief efforts. The Chinese government was lauded abroad for its swift and vigorous response to the disaster. And journalists praised the uncharacteristic "openness" to foreign media coverage of the disaster – that is, until mourning families began blaming the government for much of the destruction.

The tragedy had temporarily pulled the nation together. But it also highlighted the gap between the prosperous cities and the poor rural areas (where most of the damage occurred) and the cost of corruption. More than 7,000 shoddily-built schools had collapsed during the earthquake entombing hundreds of children while reinforced government buildings sustained little damage. Media censorship was reinstituted when teachers and grieving parents (many of whom had lost their only child)[71] began questioning whether official corruption had led to faulty construction.

Olympics

On August 8, 2008 at 8:08 pm,[72] the moment the Chinese government and much of the world had been waiting for finally arrived. Two thousand and eight illuminated Fou drummers opened one of the most spectacular Olympics productions in history. Although there were a few incidents (sales of fraudulent tickets, the stabbing of an American visitor by a disturbed Chinese assailant, accounts of restrictions on journalists and accusations that China's Olympic gymnasts were underage), the Olympic games went relatively smoothly. China won the most gold medals (51) although the United States won the largest number of medals overall (110 including eight won by swimmer Michael Phelps).

2008 Financial Crisis

The glow enjoyed throughout the Summer Olympic Games dimmed by the end of 2008 as China began to feel the effects of the global financial crisis. In order to absorb more than 20 million new entrants into the country's labor force annually, China's export-driven economy needed to maintain 9-10% growth. But with sales to financially-strapped U.S. and European consumers declining, China's economic growth also dropped causing rising unemployment and other social pressures. Like the U.S., Britain and other countries, the Chinese government attempted to forestall disaster by cutting interest rates and issuing trillion dollar stimulus packages. But in spite of the government's great push to become integrated with the rest of the world (via membership in the IMF and as host of the Olympics) China would also be fated to suffer with the rest of the world during periods of economic slumps.

---

[71] In order to keep the exploding population in check, the Chinese government enacted a law in 1979 that only permitted Chinese people to have only one child or face penalties. Exceptions were made for peasants and minority groups (see page 90).

[72] In Chinese, the word for "8" sounds like the word for "prosperity" and hence is considered lucky.

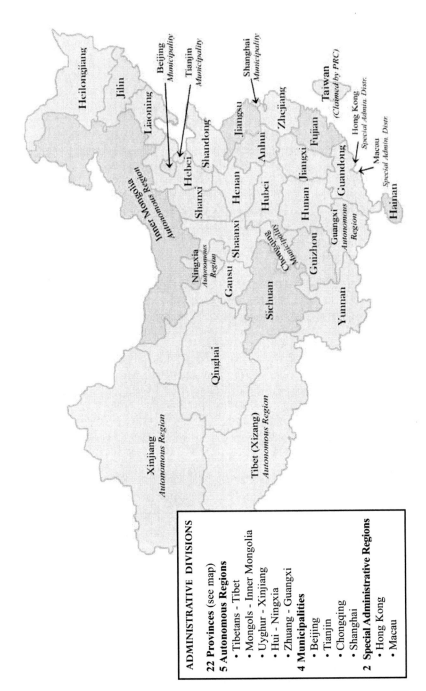

ADMINISTRATIVE DIVISIONS

22 Provinces (see map)
5 Autonomous Regions
- Tibetans - Tibet
- Mongols - Inner Mongolia
- Uyghur - Xinjiang
- Hui - Ningxia
- Zhuang - Guangxi
4 Municipalities
- Beijing
- Tianjin
- Chongqing
- Shanghai
2 Special Administrative Regions
- Hong Kong
- Macau

GOVERNMENT

China's state constitution describes the country's government as "socialist" with "all power belonging to the people" (Article 2). This power is exercised through representation in the **National People's Congress**, which is constitutionally deemed the "highest organ of state power" (Article 57), and local People's Congresses which are decided through democratic elections.[73]

In practice, however, the highest organ of power in the PRC is the **Communist Party of China (CPC)** with the greatest authority being wielded by the nine-member **Politburo Standing Committee** and the **Party's General Secretary** (who may also hold a number of other high-ranking positions). **Hu Jintao** is China's **"paramount leader"** holding the posts of **CPC General Secretary** (since 2002), **President** (since 2003) and **Chairman of the Central Military Commission** (since 2004). He is expected to hold these posts until the 18th **National Congress of the Communist Party of China** to be held in 2012.

COMMUNIST PARTY OF CHINA (CPC or CCP)

Founded in 1921, the Communist Party of China is the world's largest political party (with almost 70 million members) and carries supreme authority in China. Unlike the United States where Americans simply choose which party they'd like to join, the Chinese have to be invited to join the Communist Party by other members and then must be approved after a trial period. Membership in the party can offer political and social advantages such as access to better schools and jobs.

After a series of disastrous campaigns (the 1957 Hundred Flowers Campaign, the 1958 Great Leap Forward and the 1966 Cultural Revolution), Mao Zedong's death in 1976 and the arrest of the corrupt Gang of Four in 1981, efforts were made to reform the government to separate the powers of the Communist Party and the State. According to the 1982 Constitution, the Communist Party (led by the General Secretary) develops policy and the State (headed by the President formally elected by the National People's Congress) would carry it out.

NATIONAL COMMUNIST PARTY CONGRESS

More than 2,000 delegates from the Communist Party meet once every five years at the **National Party Congress** to make changes to the Communist Party Constitution and elect the Party's roughly 300-member **Central Committee.** The Central Committee, in turn, elects the 24-member **Politburo**, the Politburo **Standing Committee** and the **General Secretary.**

---

[73]According to government figures, since 1988 village elections for local chairmen and other posts have been conducted in more than 600,000 communities under the supervision of local branches of the Communist Party. Delegates to People's Congresses at city or county level are directly elected by constituents.

POLITBURO STANDING COMMITTEE

The top leadership in the Communist Party sits on the Standing Committee, a 5-9 member "inner cabinet" that is formally chosen by the Central Committee (although in practice, preselected by top officials). The Standing Committee is headed by the **General Secretary** of the Communist Party, the highest ranking official in China (currently held by Hu Jintao).

POLITBURO (Political Bureau)

The members of the Standing Committee are also members of the 24-member Politburo which generally also includes General Secretaries from important provinces and municipalities like Shanghai and Beijing. The Politburo meets once a month to discuss all important issues and make decisions.

NATIONAL PEOPLE'S CONGRESS (NPC)

The National People's Congress, the country's legislative branch, is officially China's highest organ of state power (according to the 1982 PRC Constitution). Members of the roughly 3,000-member body (most are also members of the Communist Party) come from China's provinces, municipalities, autonomous regions and the armed forces to officially make and enact laws. The National People's Congress also "elects" and can remove the country's president and vice-president, the Chairman of the Central Military Commission and the head of the Supreme Court – although, again, these positions and the laws that pass through the congress have largely been pre-decided by important Communist Party leaders.

The Standing Committee of the NPC (directed by a Chairman) supplements, amends and interprets laws when the National People's Congress is not in session and supervises the work of the State Council, the Central Military Commission and the Supreme People's Court among other things.

The National People's Congress has the reputation for acting as a rubber-stamping organization for the Communist Party but, increasingly, NPC members have been exercising their constitutional rights under Article 73 (the right to question) and Article 75 (legal immunity of speeches in Congress) to speak out at meetings and cast negative votes.

PRESIDENT

China's President is formally the Head-of-State with the power to declare war and a state of emergency. The President also appoints the Premier, Vice-Premiers, State Councilor and Ministers and is responsible for China's foreign affairs. Mao Zedong exercised the powers of Head-of-State until 1959 when, in the wake of the disastrous Great Leap Forward, the presidency passed to **Liu Shaoqi**. For a few years, Liu Shaoqi, **Deng Xiaoping** and **Zhou Enlai** exercised governmental power and began enacting economic reforms. But the post of President became vacant again after Liu Shaoqi was accused of being a "Capitalist-roader" and subsequently jailed (he died in prison in 1969). Mao

Zedong regained power after launching the 1966 Cultural Revolution.

The position of President was revived again in 1982, at first ceremonially held by **Soong Chingling**, the widow of Sun Yat-sen, and then by **Li Xiannian** (1983-1988) and then **Yang Shangkun** (1988-1992) – but real power was wielded by the paramount leader, **Deng Xiaoping**, who held the posts of General Secretary of the Communist Party of China <u>and</u> Premier. After Yang Shankun was removed from power in 1992, the General Secretary of the Chinese Communist Party, **Jiang Zemin**, became President thereby formally joining the State and Party sections of government.[74]

Rank of Leadership
1. Paramount Leader
2. General Secretary of the CPC
3. President
4. Chairman of the NPC
5. Premier
6. Chairman of the CMC

PREMIER
The **Premier** heads the 50-member **State Council** or **Central People's Government of the People's Republic of China**, the highest organ of state administration. With the help of four Vice-Premiers, five State Councilors and the Secretary-General, the Premier oversees the work of all the ministries, commissions, departments and agencies that manage China's 4.5 million-strong central bureaucracy. The ministries administer economic affairs, urban and rural development, the affairs of education, science, culture, public health, family planning, physical culture and other civil affairs. They also conduct foreign affairs, safeguard the rights of minority nationalities and protect the rights and interests of Chinese nationals residing abroad.

CENTRAL MILITARY COMMISSION (CMC)
The Chinese Communist Party's senior leaders also head the 11-member **Military Affairs Commission** which makes all decisions regarding actions of the 2.5 million-strong **People's Liberation Army**, the **Chinese People's Armed Police Force** and the **militia** and in 2009 operated on a budget of $70 billion. China's Paramount Leader also heads the Central Military Commission (as of 2005 the Chairmanship of the CMC was held by Hu Jintao).

POWER STRUCTURE
The greatest authority comes from the paramount leader and the Standing Committee of the Communist Party. Power then trickles down from Beijing to the 22 provinces, four city governments or "Municipalities" (Beijing, Tianjin, Chongqing and Shanghai) and five autonomous regions (Tibetans, Zhuang in Guangxi, Uighurs in Xinjiang, Mongols in Inner Mongolia and Hui in Ningxia) (see map pg. 57). From the provinces, authority passes down to the prefectures, the counties, towns and then villages.

---

[74] The Tiananmen Square incident, the political and economic turmoil taking place in Eastern Europe and Russia in the late 1980s and Soviet leader Mikhail Gorbachev's introduction of reforms (dubbed *Perestroika* or "restructuring") that called for the separation of powers and weaker party control of the Soviet government motivated China's leaders to strengthen their hold on government.

CHINA'S LEADERSHIP

Paramount Leader[a]
Mao Zedong	1949-1976
Hua Guofeng	1976-1981
Deng Xiaoping	1981-1989
Jiang Zemin	1989-2004
Hu Jintao	2004-

Chairman of the Communist Party of China (CPC)[b]
Mao Zedong	1943-1976
Hua Guofeng	1976-1981
Hu Yaobang	1981-1982

General Secretary of Communist Party of China (CPC)
Mao Zedong	1943-1956[c]
Deng Xiaoping	1956-1967[d]
Hu Yaobang	1980-1987
Zhao Ziyang	1987-1989
Jiang Zemin	1989-2002
Hu Jintao	2002-

President of the People's Republic of China (PRC)
Mao Zedong	1949-1959
Liu Shaoqi	1959-1968
Li Xiannian	1983-1988
Yang Shangkun	1988-1993
Jiang Zemin	1993-2003
Hu Jintao	2003 -

Premier of the People's Republic of China (PRC)
Zhou Enlai	1949-1976
Hua Guofeng	1976-1980
Zhao Ziyang	1983-1987
Li Peng	1988-1998
Wen Jiabao	2003-

Chairman of the Central Military Commission (CMC)
Mao Zedong	1954-1976
Hua Guofeng	1976-1981
Deng Xiaoping	1981-1989
Jiang Zemin	1990-2005
Hu Jintao	2005-

[a] The Paramount Leader holds the greatest power over the Communist Party of China, the Central People's Government and the People's Liberation Army

[b] This post was abolished in 1982.

[c] After 1956 the General Secretary exercised day-to-day management of the Party while the Chairman retained control over the Politburo.

[d] The post of General Secretary of the CPC was left vacant from 1967-1980.

ECONOMY

In just three decades, China evolved from being a financially insignificant nation into the world's third largest economy with an average growth of about 9% a year (by contrast, the U.S. economy grows on average by 3% a year). More than three-quarters of all new toys and a third of all shoes in the world are made in China and the nation is a leading exporter of automobile parts, computers and other electronics, household goods, and clothing.

One reason for China's global economic success is the country's great supply of cheap labor. Income in China is far below that of Europe, the United States and other parts of Asia. China's GDP per capita is estimated to be $6,000 while the average American income is $47,000 a year, for example. However salaries earned by urban workers in China have increased threefold since 1978 and rural incomes have increased fivefold. The rapid rise has been dubbed the "**Chinese Miracle**" and is considered remarkable since the growth was not the result of natural market forces but was orchestrated by China's authoritarian government.

BACKGROUND
Mao Zedong
Like the Soviet leaders **Vladimir Lenin** (r. 1917-1924) and **Joseph Stalin** (r. 1922-1953), China's communist leader Mao Zedong set out in 1949 to create an egalitarian communist utopia in China based on the theories of German philosopher **Karl Marx**. Mao, however, deviated from Marx's theory that communism would result after the industrial workers (or "proletariat") took over the "means of production"[75] from the ruling capitalist classes (that is, the workers would take over industries and share profits). Instead, Mao concentrated industrial workers but on China's hundreds of millions of agricultural peasants. These peasants, it was theorized, would be instrumental in guiding China toward an ideal Communist society where all people are equal and property is owned in common by the population. They would become the leaders of the communist revolution.

After the Chinese Communist Party defeated the **Kuomintang Nationalists** (see pg. 36), (who, Mao said, had replaced the old warlords with new ones who subjected the working class and peasantry to even more ruthless exploitation and oppression) social and economic changes were enacted that reflected Mao Zedong's communist ambitions.

Agricultural Reforms
In 1955 farmers were no longer allowed to own land privately. Instead they were expected to join "collective farms" that were managed by several families under state supervision. In 1958 during the "Great Leap Forward," dozens of collectives were joined together to form **communes**. The members of the communes (sometimes 10,000 families) were organized into "**production

---

[75] The "means of production" are the things needed to produce something including labor, tools, machinery etc.

brigades" and shared everything. All the commune members ate together in giant mess halls, the children were sent to communal nurseries and schools,[76] and medical care and other necessities were all provided.

Crops that were not consumed by commune families were turned over to the state which would then distribute the food to city-dwellers. A quota system was set up to determine how much each commune could contribute to the state based on the output of the farms, and members were encouraged to try to exceed the goal as much as possible.

Along with agricultural success, Mao hoped to transform China into an industrial power that would rival Britain. In order to accomplish this, families in the communes were expected to contribute their time and all the metal they possessed including pots and pans, tools, bicycles etc., to be melted down in large, but inefficient **"backyard furnaces."**[77] Rather than producing high-quality steel, though, most of the backyard furnaces produced unus-

---

SOCIALIST TERMS

Bourgeoisie: Members of the property-owning class. Capitalists.

Proletariat: The working classes

Capitalism: In a capitalist society, a small group of people (the bourgeoisie) own property and businesses and hire others (the proletariat) to do the work.

Communism: Communism is an ideal, utopian system in which all the people jointly own all property and businesses and decide, democratically, what should be produced, how everyone should contribute and how the products and profits will be distributed.

Socialism: Socialism is a transitional stage between capitalism and communism when the working class (the proletariat) takes over leadership from the bourgeoisie (the owning classes) creating a "dictatorship of the proletariat."

"Dictatorship of the Proletariat": A government led by the people (or workers) as opposed to one that is led by a smaller number of "bourgeoisie."

Karl Marx (1818-1883): A German philosopher who held that the proletariat (which did all the work) was being exploited by members of the owning, capitalist class (the "bourgeoisie"). He believed that mankind would only be "free" when the members of the working classes took control of the "means of production" (the factories, tools etc.) thereby eliminating any need for the bourgeoisie. Marx believed this change would happen naturally as a result of growing tension between workers and owners.

Vladimir Illyich Lenin (1870-1924): Lenin, like Marx, also held that the workers were entitled to control the "means of production." Unlike Marx, however, Lenin believed that this could only be accomplished by force via a proletariat revolution. Lenin became one of the principle leaders of the Russian October (or "Bolshevik") Revolution in 1917 that overthrew the Russian ruling party.

---

[76] Along with trying to destroy individualism (considered a product of capitalism), the Communist Party attempted to break up family units hoping to foster loyalty to the Party.

[77] An estimated 600,000 commune steel producing factories were established in China between 1958 and 1959. Other communes produced fertilizers, pesticides, building materials and other products.

GDP Growth	
1957	5.1
1958	21.3 [a]
1959	8.8
1960	- 0.3 [b]
1961	-27.3 [b]
1963	10.2 [c]
1964	18.3 [c]
1967	-5.7 [d]
1968	-4.1 [d]
1969	16.9 [e]
1970	19.4 [e]
1971	7.0
1972	3.8 [f]
1974	2.3 [f]
1975	8.7
1976	-1.6 [g]
1977	7.6
1978	11.7 [h]
1982	9.1
1984	15.2 [i]
1985	13.5
1989	4.1 [j]
1992	14.2 [k]
2003	10.0
2007	11.4

[a] Great Leap Forward, numbers were exaggerated.

[b] Consequences of Great Leap Forward.

[c] Temporary relaxation under Deng Xiaoping and Liu Shaoqi

[d] Cultural Revolution.

[e] Restoration of order after Cultural Revolution.

[f] Gang of Four vs. Zhou Enlai.

[g] Earthquakes, drought and death of Mao Zedong.

[h] Communes dissolved. Family farming encouraged.

[i] Opening of first SEZs.

[j] Tiananmen Square massacre. Foreign investments drop.

[k] Deng takes tour of south. Increased investment in SEZs.

able low-grade metal or "slag." Furniture was sacrificed and forests were denuded to provide firewood to heat the furnaces. Agricultural tools were melted for the cause. And with so many field workers being taken off farm duty to work in the "steel mills," fewer were left to tend the fields leading to smaller harvests.

Making matters worse, many village leaders, eager to make a good impression, falsely reported higher yields than their communes had actually produced. The inflated numbers meant the communes were committed to contributing even higher percentages of their crops to the state leaving some villages with little left over for their own consumption. For a period of time, China was actually exporting agricultural products while tens of millions of people living in rural areas starved to death.

Urban Reforms
In the cities, all enterprises were publicly owned and managed by the central government. Prices and wages were determined by the state and profits were submitted to the government for redistribution. Workers were assigned to their jobs based on their education and skills and could expect to be employed by the same state-run company in the same city for the rest of their lives. (This kind of guaranteed job security has been termed the "**iron rice bowl**").

The system, while originally intended to ensure a more equitable distribution of wealth, led to stagnation. City workers who were guaranteed incomes no matter how they performed were not motivated to be productive and the central government made unwise management decisions.

China's communist party had the task of employing, managing and feeding a billion-strong population that was growing at a rate of 47%. But less than a decade after the country recovered from the grain crisis and ensuing famine in the late 50s, Mao Zedong launched a "cultural revolution" to reinforce China's commitment to communism. Mao was motivated by fear that China would follow the Soviet Union's direction away from communism (he accused General Secretary of the Soviet Communist Party **Nikita Khrushchev** of replacing the "dictatorship of the proletariat" with a "dictatorship of the privileged, Soviet bourgeois clique"),[78] and fear that he was being overshadowed by other Chinese Communist Party cadres.[79]

In the course of the **Cultural Revolution**, contact with the outside world was severed. Books, artwork, religious institutions and other symbols of "superstition," the capitalist West or the bourgeoisie were zealously destroyed by roving Red Guards. Schools and universities were closed. The government fell into disarray due to bloody purges of political rivals. And the economy was in shambles.

The Great Proletarian Cultural Revolution officially ended in 1969 but Mao Zedong retained ultimate power until his death in 1976.

Deng Xiaoping

Deng Xiaoping, one of the original participants in the young Chinese Communist Party's Long March in the 1930s, won enough of Mao Zedong's trust to be appointed General Secretary of the Communist Party Central Committee in 1956. But Deng favored a more practical approach to governance than the more radical Chairman Mao.

In the wake of the catastrophic **Great Leap Forward** (dubbed the "Three Difficult Years" from 1958-1962), Mao was forced to keep a low profile while Deng Xiaoping and President Liu Shaoqi took charge of the daily affairs of the state. During this period of political relaxation, Deng attempted to make changes in the agricultural system giving peasants greater incentives to increase production. To justify the deviation from earlier communist policies, Deng Xiaoping maintained that "it doesn't matter if the cat is yellow[80] or black as long as it catches the mouse."

In August 1966, Mao Zedong, seeing his power wane, warned in a speech that there were people in power who were "enforcing a bourgeois dictatorship" and were intent on sabotaging the "great revolution of the proletariat."

---

[78] When Khrushchev became General Secretary of the U.S.S.R. in 1953 he began a de-Stalinization campaign denouncing the Soviet Union's former General Secretary, Joseph Stalin. He also promoted peaceful coexistence with the West (which Mao called "colluding with U.S. Imperialists) and pulled back from Stalin's socialist agricultural planning and other reforms

[79] In 1962 while Mao was on a trip, Deng Xiaoping, Zhou Enlai and Liu Shaoqi held a conference denouncing "leftists" in direct contrast to Mao's 1959 campaign against "rightists."

[80] The color of the cat in the statement which foreshadowed Deng's departure from communism when he became China's leader in the 1980s, was later changed from yellow to white.

Soon after Mao's **"Bombard the Headquarters"** speech, as it was called, Deng Xiaoping was expelled from the government and sent to work at a tractor factory. His son was imprisoned and tortured.

By Premier Zhou Enlai's invitation, Deng was "rehabilitated" in 1973 after "admitting" to having been a "capitalist roader" (see pg. 43). But Mao could not tolerate Deng's independence. Soon after Zhou Enlai's death in 1976, Deng Xiaoping was again purged from the government and spent the next few months under house arrest.

Mao Zedong's Death
Even after Mao's death, his influence continued under the banner of the **"two whatevers"** (following *whatever* Mao said and *whatever* instructions he gave) held up by Mao's successor **Hua Guofeng**. But the vast majority of China's population was desperately poor, weary of the archaic working conditions in the communes and in the factories and tired of Maoist policies.

In this atmosphere, Deng Xiaoping's December 1978 proclamation that "we need to alter China's backward state, move forward and build our country into a strong and modernized socialist state" was more fitting to the times.

As Deng climbed back up the political ladder, he was careful not to completely repudiate the ideals of the Communist Party nor entirely besmirch the memory of the PRC's founding father (Mao's body is still enshrined and on display in Beijing). He criticized the Cultural Revolution[81] but not its architect, assessing that Mao Zedong had been "seven parts good and three parts bad." Deng Xiaoping continued to uphold socialism albeit with "Chinese Characteristics" which, to Deng, meant eradicating poverty.

REFORMS (1980s)
Rural Reforms

> "Socialism means eliminating poverty. Pauperism is not socialism, still less communism."
>
> **Deng Xiaoping, 1984**

As in the early days of the People's Republic of China, reform under the direction of Deng Xiaoping began in the countryside. Land from the collective farms was redistributed to households who could choose what crops they would grow – or even whether to continue farming or enter another profession (called the **"household-responsibility system"**). Small privately owned shops, stands and other businesses run by former farmers or as supplemental income, sprung up in the countryside providing goods and services that had not been previously available in the countryside.

Farmers who continued to work the land were still required to fill govern-

---

[81] For a short time during the "Beijing Spring" in the late 1970s, Deng Xiaoping permitted criticism of the government's previous mistakes and excesses by inviting the general public to record their thoughts on the Democracy Wall in Beijing. But the experiment came to an end in 1979 when dissenters began targeting the current regime. (See pg. 45)

ment quotas but could keep the profits from excess crops they sold on the open market. Eventually the quota system was replaced by taxes.

Peasants saw their incomes rise by about 15% per year as a result of the reforms and productivity increased along with the standard-of-living.

Urban Reforms
Workers in the cities were also permitted to set up small privately owned enterprises like food stands, repair shops or service-oriented businesses – but the vast majority of people continued to work in **state-owned enterprises (SOEs)** which provided housing, schooling, stability and other perks.

In the early 1980s, the government began reforming poorly managed, unprofitable and wasteful state-owned enterprises. Under Mao Zedong, state-run businesses were expected to remit all profits to the state and could expect a bailout if there were losses. Under Deng Xiaoping, incentives were created by giving managers more authority and allowing enterprises to keep some of their profits to reinvest into the business, upgrade technology and equipment, give bonuses or provide collective benefits for the workers.[82]

> *"Capitalism can only enrich less than 10% of the Chinese population: it can never enrich the remaining more than 90%. But if we adhere to socialism and apply the principle of distribution to each according to his work, there will not be excessive disparities in wealth."*
>
> **Deng Xiaoping, June 1984**

In the mid 1980s, state-owned ventures that exceeded their quotas were permitted to sell their surplus products in the open market at higher rates than the state price. The businesses were also given even more autonomy to hire and fire employees, deal directly with suppliers and, in some cases, decide what products to make.

The number of state-owned industries, which once made up the vast majority of China's enterprises, dropped below 50% by the mid 1990s. The rest consisted of collective enterprises (owned by workers), town/village enterprises or "TVEs" owned by communities, and private industries – both domestic and foreign-owned.

"SPECIAL ECONOMIC ZONES" (SEZs)
Before Deng Xiaoping came to power in the late 1970s, China had very little contact with the outside world. Foreign trade, which had accounted for nearly a quarter of China's income in the 1950s, fell to about 6% in the early 1970s and few citizens or officials had been to a different country or knew how a modern, non-socialist economy worked. According to Deng Xiaoping, China's "closed-door" policy was one of the most significant reasons why China remained backwards while the rest of the developing world advanced.

---

[82] State-owned businesses that failed were still given government subsidies but in the form of a loan.

To raise China up to contemporary standards, Deng embarked on a fact-finding mission to South-East Asia soon after his "rehabilitation" in 1978, and chose **Singapore** as China's new economic model since that nation showed rapid economic growth while maintaining strict central governmental control.

After his trip, China's central government established four "**special economic zones**" – key regions where a degree of capitalism and foreign investment would be permitted – in the coastal cities of **Shenzhen, Zhuhai, Shatou** and **Xiamen**. Investors (initially primarily from Hong Kong and Taiwan) were lured by tax incentives and access to cheap labor in exchange for teaching Chinese workers new advanced techniques and technology.

In just a few years, small towns like Shenzhen (considered one of the fastest growing cities in the world) transformed into giant metropolises with skyscrapers, shopping malls, theme parks, museums, resorts and tourist attractions. New jobs were created for hundreds of thousands of Chinese citizens making some of them rich.

Fourteen additional coastal SEZs were created in 1984 – this time drawing foreign investors from the United States, Europe and other Asian countries. More were created along the Yangtze River and in Hainan (the entire island was turned into an SEZ in 1988) as well as in other areas in subsequent years.

RESULTS

Within three decades, China experienced spectacular economic growth. Farmers saw their incomes increase fivefold while urban dwellers' incomes tripled. And although the population of rural workers had shrunk from 82% in 1978 to 55% in 2007, grain output nearly doubled, cotton output tripled, beet-root crops quadrupled and sugar cane output increased five times.[83]

Foreign exports grew from about 9 billion U.S. dollars in 1978 to more than a trillion dollars in 2008 and China's GDP (gross domestic product[84]) quadrupled. Access to tap water increased sixfold. There were more than twelve times more paved roads and sewer pipelines and fifteen times more public vehicles on the road than there were in the late 1970s.

---

[83] Numbers based on the 1978 and 2008 Chinese Statistical Yearbooks.

[84] The GDP is the measurement of the total market value of goods and services produced in a country in a given year.

Almost all Chinese citizens saw a great increase in their standards of living since the 1970s but the growth also created a large and widening gap between rural and urban incomes and services. Urban workers on average earned more than three times what rural workers earned – a difference that reached about $1,600 per year per person in 2008 according to Agricultural Ministry statistics. Rural towns also had poorer schools, fewer retirement benefits and inferior health care and other services than their urban counterparts despite the central government's attempts to bridge the gap between wealthy coastal cities and China's interior by pouring money into less economically successful regions.[85]

With the dismantling of the communes and the lifting of travel restrictions,[86] hundreds of millions of former farmers made their way to the cities to seek fortunes and opportunities working for private companies, doing construction, or selling goods and services on city streets. Most of the migrant workers put up with substandard living conditions and social isolation in order to earn twice or more what they could back in their home villages.

To try to ease congestion and trim the glut of workers in the city, the Central Government constructed roads and railroads from coastal regions to the interior of China and encouraged wealthier Chinese and foreign investors to "go west."[87] But the very "un-socialist" disparity between the haves and the have-nots and growing unemployment (worsened by layoffs resulting from the drop in exports due to the 2008 global economic crisis), both sources of periodic unrest, are of great concern to the regime.

GLOBAL ECONOMIC CRISIS 2008

Since 1978, China's economy has grown at an average rate of 9% a year. The country has maintained this growth in part by keeping the value of the Chinese currency, the *yuan* (or *renminbi, RMB*), low against the dollar and euro. As long as the *yuan* is less valuable than foreign currencies, Chinese wages are low (which encourages foreign companies to build factories in China in order to take advantage of cheap local labor) and imports are expensive (discouraging Chinese citizens from buying goods made abroad). For that reason, China exports more goods than it imports, earning the country surplus cash.

In order to prevent inflation[88] the Chinese government has invested much of its surplus cash, more than $700 billion worth, in United States Treasury

[85] Through programs like the "China Western Development Strategy" (2000), "Revitalize Northeast China Initiative" (2003) and "Rise of Central China Policy" (2004), the government attempted to accelerate regional development by improving schools, restructuring state-owned enterprises, stepping up environmental protection efforts, developing telecommunication systems, hydropower plants and other construction projects.

[86] Until 1980, migration between cities was nearly impossible since food rations, education and jobs were allocated based on citizens' registered residence.

[87] The migration of Han Chinese to cities in the west created some problems in places like Lhasa, Tibet and cities in Xinjiang where local cultures were overtaken by Chinese businesses.

[88] More money in circulation results in higher prices or "inflation."

Bonds [89] making China the largest holder of U.S. debt in the world. The relationship closely ties the two countries together: if China decides to withdraw its "loan" or stops buying bonds, the U.S. economy could collapse; but since China relies so heavily on U.S. investors and the American market to sell its goods, a U.S. economic collapse would essentially destroy China's economy.

The intertwined economic relationship between China and the U.S. (as well as Europe, Japan and other nations), was also demonstrated during the 2008 global economic crisis. When America's purchasing power declined, China's economy suffered. Fewer Chinese-made products were sold abroad causing factories to close and unemployment to rise. The crisis caused a panic in China which must maintain a 9% growth in order to create jobs for the millions of Chinese entering the workforce every year.

To forestall an economic disaster, the Chinese government, like that of the United States, Japan and European nations, invested hundreds of billions of dollars into its own economy to stimulate growth. But despite the government's efforts, China's GDP growth slowed to just over 6% by March 2009, the country's lowest rate in 20 years.

HONG KONG

Following the Opium war in 1842, China under the Qing regime signed three treaties that would eventually cede all of Hong Kong to the British Empire. The first two gave the British control over the **island of Hong Kong** (1842) and the **Kowloon Peninsula** (1860) "in perpetuity." The third treaty in 1898 ceded the **New Territories**, the area that adjoins China, to the British government for 99 years – a lease that expired on June 30,1997.

Under British control, Hong Kong evolved from a sparsely populated region that served as a base for British naval and military operations in East Asia to an international financial center that would compete with Japan, Singapore, South Korea and the other economic "**Asian Tiger**," Taiwan.

Background

In the first decade under British rule, Hong Kong was overshadowed by commercial success in China's Guangdong (Canton) province and Shanghai.

---

[89] U.S. Treasury Bonds are issued by the U.S. government to raise money. Buyers earn interest on the bonds and cannot recall them until their "date of maturity" (usually 10 years). U.S. Treasury Bonds are considered very safe since they are backed by the powerful Federal Reserve.

But its status slowly began to change during the civil war between the KMT Nationalists and Mao Zedong's Communists when businessmen and their families began to migrate to Hong Kong to avoid the prospect of life under Communist rule. The migration of skilled workers and their capital continued after the establishment of the People's Republic of China in 1949.

In the 1950s, Hong Kong's revenue stream came from commerce through its free port. In the 1960s, the British colony concentrated on industry manufacturing cheap consumer goods, appliances and electronics. When manufacturers began moving their factories to other Asian countries that offered cheaper labor, Hong Kong turned to finance. But Hong Kong's businessmen soon returned to manufacturing – this time relying on cheap labor available in neighboring Guangdong Province in China. Eventually, millions of Chinese were employed in thousands of Hong Kong-owned factories in the Guangdong province and other parts of China and the Chinese invested millions of dollars in Hong Kong linking the two countries economically.

As 1997 approached, the British (represented by Prime Minister **Margaret Thatcher**) and Chinese leader **Deng Xiaoping** began discussing plans to return the New Territories to the PRC as agreed in the 1898 treaty. It was decided that without the New Territories, the island of Hong Kong and Kowloon would not be economically viable so they, too, would be returned to Chinese control in 1997.

In the interest of China, Britain, and Hong Kong's residents, Hong Kong would be permitted to maintain its economic and political systems for fifty years under the "**one country, two systems**"[90] arrangement. As a "**Special Administrative Region**" (SAR) Hong Kong, as well as SAR **Macao** (also returned to China in 1999) would be permitted to maintain its own currency and conduct its own domestic affairs but would have to rely on the PRC for national defense and diplomatic relations.

Today, the modern metropolis of Hong Kong, now governed by a Chinese representative, is considered one of the freest capitalist economies in the world housing the 6th largest stock exchange in the world and maintaining a GDP per capita that is comparable to that of the United States. (Hong Kong's GDP per capita is $43,800, the U.S. GDP per capita is $47,000). More than a third of China's companies are listed on Hong Kong's stock exchange earning China more than $160 billion in stock offerings in the past ten years. Most of Guandong's exports go through Hong Kong and trade between mainland China and Hong Kong accounts for nearly 50% of Hong Kong's exports and imports.

---

[90] Hong Kong and other Special Administrative Regions in the "one country, two systems" arrangement would remain capitalistic while the rest of China would continue to do business within China's socialist system.

RELIGION AND PHILOSOPHIES

Mao Zedong, like his communist predecessors (**Karl Marx, Vladimir Lenin** *et al.*), viewed religion as a poisonous opiate[91] of the people. The Chinese Communist Party further objected to any institution or ideology that might direct authority away from the party, especially those religions practiced and utilized by colonialists to infiltrate China during the Qing Dynasty.

The attack on religion was particularly vicious during the **Cultural Revolution** when the state encouraged people to destroy all things that represented Old Habits, Old Ideas, Old Culture, Old Customs (the "**Four Olds**") as well as vestiges of imperialism. Thousands of temples, mosques and churches were destroyed between 1966 and 1967, clerics of all religions were attacked and arrested and believers were publicly humiliated. The aim was to completely eradicate religion and replace it with blind devotion to the Chinese Communist Party, reverence for its leader, Mao Zedong, and adherence to the party's doctrine as it had been laid out in Mao's "Little Red Book."

After the destructive fervor of the Cultural Revolution had subsided, the Party slowly began to tolerate strictly controlled religious worship so as to prevent believers from gathering underground.

When Deng Xiaoping came to power in the 1980s, the government codified the country's new openness by including the right to religious belief in the PRC's 1982 constitution, albeit with conditions: religious activity could not "disrupt public order, impair the health of citizens or interfere with the educational system of the state" nor could it be "subject to any foreign domination."

Although Catholicism was among five religions recognized by the state (the others are Buddhism, Daoism, Islam and Protestantism), **Roman Catholics** in China who defer to the spiritual authority of the Pope are considered in violation of the constitutional clause that outlaws adherence to religions that are "subject to foreign domination." **Falun Gong** (see pg. 78) was also condemned because the religion allegedly "disrupted public order" and "impaired the health of citizens" by implying that practitioners could be healed of illnesses if they correctly performed certain rituals. (Indeed some Falun Gong members turned to the religion instead of seeking expensive medical treatments.)

To ensure that religious institutions operated within the law, the government set up a registration system. Churches, mosques or temples that did not register with the appropriate ministry could be subject to legal action while the offending members of the congregation risked fines or imprisonment.

---

[91] Religion, according to German philosopher Karl Marx, creates the illusion of a better world after death. For the poor, this "fantasy" was preferable to the reality of their impoverished lives. Religion, to them, was a relief just like opiate drugs relieve physical pain. As long as religion is available as an "escape" from social ills, he theorized, sufferers will not address nor solve social ills.

Sanctioned religions in China are protected, organized and monitored by seven national religious associations (China Daoist Association, Buddhist Association of China, Islamic Association of China, Chinese Christian Council, Patriotic Association of the Catholic Church in China, Chinese Bishops College and the Three-Self Patriotic Movement Committee of the Protestant Churches of China), and hundreds of local organizations and colleges.

DAOISM (TAOISM)

Daoism offered relief for believers during China's tumultuous and chaotic "Spring and Autumn Period" by suggesting that mankind should accept life's circumstances, yield to the natural order of the universe and live in harmony with nature. As a philosophy of "escape," Daoism advocated detaching oneself from world events.

Daoism's primary scripture, the **Dao De Ching**, is attributed to **Lao Zi** (literally "Old Master"), a hermit who lived either in the 6th or 4th centuries B.C. during the time of the **Hundred Schools of Thought**. (see pg. 4)

According to the Daoist philosophy, natural order is maintained by the flow of "*qi*" or "spiritual energy," and balanced by the opposing yet complementary dual forces of *Yin* (symbolized as darkness or winter) and *Yang* (light or summer).

Man can ensure that *qi* is not disrupted by exercising moderation, compassion and humility. One can also maintain the positive flow of *qi* in the home by arranging furniture and other objects according to the principals of **Feng Shui** (literally "wind, water"), an ancient Chinese system of esthetics that draws on the laws of astronomy, geomagnetism (which is based on the polarity of *Yin Yang*) and other natural forces. According to practitioners of Chinese medicine, obstructions in the flow of *qi* through the body can cause many kinds of illnesses that can be cured or alleviated by unblocking the obstruction through **acupuncture**, herbal medicines and special exercises.

The practice of **Qigong**, a slow rhythmic routine of movement and breathing exercises performed daily primarily by the elderly in China, is said to improve health by enhancing the circulation of *qi* in the body.

CONFUCIANISM

Like Lao Zi, **Kong Fu Zi** (literally "Venerable Master Kong") or **Confucius** also advocated adherence to the law of order. Confucius (born in 551 BC) and his disciples, however, focused on the hierarchy of "social" order: between father and son; husband and wife; older brother to younger brother; friend to friend and ruler to ruled. According to Confucius, peace and stability resulted when men, women and children maintained deep respect and deference to their superiors (i.e. employee to employer, son to father) who, in turn, were encouraged to act benevolently toward their subordinates. A kind ruler, it was reasoned, would be respected and loved by his people who would reciprocate by remaining loyal, orderly and obedient.

The tenets and lessons of Confucius teachings including ideals of ancestor worship, respect for elders, family loyalty and the principle that "you should not do to others what you do not want done to yourself" were organized into **The Analects of Confucius** by his disciples.

MOHISM
Soon after the death of Confucius, **Mozi** (or Mo-Tzu) (470 B.C. - 391 B.C.), like the other philosophers born during the chaos and violence in the Warring States Period, sought to create a more peaceful and organized society based on respect and universal love. He emphasized self-reflection and authenticity rather than obedience to ritual. Mozi and his followers abhorred war (except in defense) and criticized opulence and frivolous pursuits. Music and lengthy, elaborate funerals, for instance, were condemned because they took time away from practical tasks like tending crops.

In order for a society to function effectively, Mozi theorized, the ruler must love all people and promote ministers according to talent rather than who they were related to. An unrighteous ruler, it was believed, would be punished by the spirits.

LEGALISM
According to the **Legalist** philosophy (as outlined by **Master Han Fei** born c. 280 B.C), benevolent rulers would spoil the people and create a weak and ineffectual state as a result. Instead, rulers had to be strict and command respect and obedience from the people in order to keep order.

Since common people are fundamentally evil and stupid, in the opinion of the Legalists, they must be controlled through strict laws and the fear of harsh punishments. Only when the rights of the individual are completely subordinated to the interests of the state can a nation be strong enough to conquer smaller states.

That is exactly what happened in 221 B.C. under the totalitarian rule of **Qin Shi Huang Di**, the first emperor of the Qin Dynasty. (See pg. 5)

BUDDHISM
According to tradition, the tenets of Buddhism arose from the example and lessons of a prince called **Siddhartha Gautama**. Siddhartha was born in 563 BC in northeast India (present-day Nepal) and, for the first three decades of his life, enjoyed a life of luxury in his

father's castle. When he turned 29, though, Siddhartha wanted to experience life beyond the confines of the palace. As he journeyed into the real world for the first time, he saw suffering, old age and death. The stark contrast to his own experiences led him on a quest to understand the human condition. After years of meditation and spiritual guidance, Siddhartha finally grasped the basic truths of human life and became enlightened. "Buddha" or "The Enlightened One" as he would then be called, spent the next 45 years traveling through India guiding others along the virtuous path that led him to achieve his elevated state of consciousness.

After his death, Buddha's message continued to spread through India, Afghanistan and Sri Lanka under Mauryan king **Ashoka** (r. 273-232 BC), and to China, Tibet and Burma in the 2nd century A.D. through monks dispatched by **Kanishka**,(r. A.D. 127-151) the king of the Kushan Empire. From China, Buddhism spread to Vietnam, Korea, Japan and other parts of Asia.

In the course of his spiritual journey, Buddha came to the conclusion that suffering exists in this world because of our attachments to things that are impermanent. Since all things are impermanent, including our own lives, we will always be frustrated unless we give up those attachments and desires.

The concept of individual spiritual enlightenment through the release of desires and relationships contradicted principles of Confucianism that promoted strong familial and societal obligations, obedience to the emperor and ancestor worship. Although Buddhism was adopted by some of China's leaders, most evidently demonstrated through the construction of more than 100,000 Buddhist statues in the Longmen Caves begun in 493, Buddhism never reached the widespread popularity that Confucianism and Daoism enjoyed in China.

ISLAM

The religion of Islam developed in Arabia in the 7th century following the transmission of a series of messages from God to Islam's Prophet Muhammad.[92] According to Muslims, these messages were similar to those received by Jesus, Moses and other prophets who preceded Muhammad, advising all people to be benevolent and submissive to God. Islam, therefore, is considered a continuation of the other two "Abrahamic" religions, Judaism and Christianity.

All Muslims must testify that there is no god but God (Allah). They are required to pray daily towards Mecca in present-day Saudi Arabia and make at least one pilgrimage to the holy city of Mecca in their lifetime (a journey called the "*hajj*"). They are encouraged to fast from sunup to sundown during the holy month of Ramadan and must make regularly contributions to charity.

---

[92] These "revelations" were later compiled into the Quran, Islam's holy book. For more about Islam please read Roraback's Islam in a Nutshell, Enisen Publishing.

After Muhammad's death in 632, Islam spread throughout Arabia, west across northern Africa to Spain, east to present-day Pakistan, and north to present-day Hungary.

The first Muslim visit to China in A.D. 651 was made by one of Muhammad's companions. China's **Tang Dynasty** Emperor **Gaozong** was purportedly so impressed with Islam that he had a mosque built in the Tang capital of Chang'an (Xi'an) which still stands today. Muslims increased among the population from that point on.

During the **Song Dynasty** (960-1279) Chinese Muslims who were connected with Islamic populations abroad dominated foreign trade and the office of Director General of Shipping was regularly held by a Muslim. The Mongols, whose empire spanned across the Islamic world, also held the Muslims in high regard during the **Yuan Dynasty** (1279-1842), elevating them to higher governmental posts than their Han Chinese counterparts. By the time of the **Ming Dynasty** (1368-1644), the Muslims were well-integrated into Chinese society, adopted Chinese names[93] and embraced some Han Chinese customs. But the golden age of Islam in China, when Nanjing had become a center of Islamic learning, ended during the **Qing Dynasty** (1644-1911). The Muslims had become victims of repressive policies and discrimination that provoked a number of revolts, the most famous being the **Dungan** or **Panthay Rebellion** of the 1800s (see pg. 22), resulting in the deaths of millions of Muslims.

Between 1912 and 1928, the Muslims (identified as Huis and Uighurs) were recognized as one of five races that made up the Chinese union, symbolized by a white stripe in the national flag flown by **Sun Yat-Sen** (the others included the Han represented by a red stripe, the Manchus [yellow], the Tibetans [black] and the Mongols [blue]). But when the communists took over in 1949, conformity to socialist principles was advocated over diversity.

Religious minorities of all denominations suffered under Mao and the Marxists, especially in the reign of terror during the Cultural Revolution, and the Muslims were no exception. More than 20,000 mosques were shut down or converted into slaughterhouses, stables or used for other purposes. Imams and Mullahs (Muslim religious leaders), accused of being feudal oppressors, were tortured or humiliated (for example by being forced to tend pig farms[94]). Islamic schools ("*madrassas*") were closed, schoolchildren were forced to attend state schools to study Marxism and hundreds of thousands of Muslims were executed.

---

[93] The family name "Fatima," the name of Muhammad's daughter, for example, was changed to "Ma" and "Muhammad" was altered to Mu or Mo.

[94] Pigs are considered unclean creatures in Islam. The consumption of pork is also forbidden.

With the death of Mao Zedong in 1976 and in light of political and social liberalization, Muslims, like all citizens of the PRC, were legally given the right to enjoy freedom of religious belief (as long as they didn't disrupt public order or undermine the authority of the state). Tens of thousands of mosques were rebuilt as a result and Chinese Muslims were again permitted to engage in Islamic practices. With relations growing between China and the oil-rich Middle Eastern countries, moreover, Chinese Muslims were actually encouraged to study Arabic (the language of the Quran) and to study in Islamic schools abroad. In 2008, direct flights from Ningxia Autonomous Region to Saudi Arabia carried a record 10,700 Chinese to perform the ritual *hajj* (although most of China's 20-35 million Muslims still cannot afford to make such a journey).

Huis and Uighurs (Uyghurs)
Among the 55 minority ethnic groups recognized by China's government, Muslims predominate in ten of them. The largest is the Hui, ethnically Han Chinese who practice Islam. The rest are primarily racially Turkish (including the Uighurs, Uzbeks, Karach, Kyrgyz, Tatars, and Dongshiang) with the greatest number living in China's "Quran Belt," **Xinjiang, Gansu, Ningxia** and **Qinghai** provinces, a sparsely populated but strategic region in northwestern China.

For the Chinese, the area is valuable because of its potential for coal mining, oil drilling and tourism. Xinjiang also has rich uranium deposits and has been used a test site for China's nuclear weapons. The Uighurs, who once made up more than 90% of Xinjiang's population, claimed the Chinese illegally occupied **East Turkestan** (as they refer to the region) in 1949 and have been steadily destroying the local culture. Indeed, since the 1950s, non-Muslim Han Chinese have been encouraged by the Central Government to

move to Xinjiang at a rate of about 200,000 people per year and have great-ly reshaped the cities economically and culturally.[95]

The influx has further inflamed the local population of Uighurs who, since the 1940s, were already engaged in periodic and sometimes violent upris-ings demanding independence and self-government. The Chinese have retal-iated by imprisoning and torturing separatists – especially after the terrorist attacks in the United State on September 11, 2001.[96]

Today China's Muslims enjoy both greater freedoms – because of China's desire to cultivate good relations with their Arab trading partners – and harsher repression – due to the perceived threat of Islamic terrorism.

FALUN GONG

In the 1990s, a new movement that combined the philosophies of Daoism and Buddhism with Chinese *qigong* breathing exercises became popular in China. **Li Hongzhi**, the founder of **Falun Gong**, or **Falun Dafa** ("Great Law Wheel"[97]) as it is known by members, maintained that practitioners could greatly improve their health and well-being by correctly channeling the *qi* through a series of meditative exercises. Performed correctly, practitioners would develop an "energy cluster" or "Falun" in their lower abdomens that cir-culated energy throughout the body by spinning in the direc-tion of the universe. The adoption of the Falun or "energy wheel," represented by a circular design of yin and yang pat-terns and swastikas,[98] became the movement's emblem, symbolically linking Falun Gong to the ancient philosophies of Daoism and Buddhism.

Adherents who cultivated their "energy wheels" through exercise, abiding by moral principles, and renouncing human desires and attachments, it was claimed, would see their gray hair turn black, their bodies heal (even from cancer) and their minds become clear.[99] Eventually, practitioners would

---

[95] Uighurs have complained about job discrimination (with the best jobs given to Han Chinese) and discriminatory laws, for example limiting Islamic sermons to be no longer than a half hour, requiring male government workers to shave their beards and female employees to remove their head scarves and forbidding Muslims under the age of 18 from attending Islamic education.

[96] More than 20 Uighur separatist "terrorists" were caught in U.S. sweeps across Pakistan and Afghanistan and subsequently detained at the U.S. prison in Guantanamo, Cuba. Some of the detainees had been receiving military training in Afghan camps to fight against Chinese rule.

[97] "Fa" denotes the principles or law of the universe. "Lun" means wheel and "Da" means great. "Gong" is the short form of the word *Qigong* or "achievement/cultivation" of "*qi*" (life energy).

[98] To Hindus, the clockwise swastika symbolizes the sun's rays and the evolution of the universe. In Buddhism it signifies eternity and universal harmony (as the balance of opposites). The swasti-ka was also adopted by ancient Greeks, Celts, Jains, Native Americans, and even Freemasons before the German Nazi's popularized it as a symbol of Aryan racial purity and white supremacy.

[99] There are also claims that practitioners can gain supernatural powers like X-ray visions and the power to walk through walls.

attain enlightenment and bodily transcendence.

The movement, which, according to Falun Gong leaders, attracted more 100 million members worldwide (Beijing claims it has no more than 2 million adherents) particularly appealed to Chinese who had become disillusioned with Marxism and the Chinese government after the 1989 Tiananmen Square incident as well as those who felt spiritually isolated by rapid market reforms.

The movement made its first appearance in 1992 when a trumpet-playing grain and oil supply clerk, **Li Hongzhi**, who, Falun Gong biographers claimed, could become invisible and levitate off the ground among other supernatural powers, began traveling through China teaching his version of Qigong. For the first few years, Li wrote and sold a number of books and videotapes to adherents and presided over mass gatherings around the country. But Falun Gong's direction changed in 1999 when a number of practitioners were beaten and arrested for gathering in protest of the publication of an article that criticized the movement.

The arrests and beatings triggered another protest by more than 10,000 Falun Gong members who assembled peacefully near a complex housing China's top leaders. The mobilization of such great numbers alarmed the government so much that it banned the group for disrupting public order, impairing the health of citizens (because practitioners were choosing Falun Gong exercises over medical care) and spreading superstition. Falun Gong members in China were subsequently persecuted, imprisoned or tortured from that point on while Li Hongzhi, branded a criminal by Chinese authorities, continued to lead the movement in exile in New York.

After the crackdown, Falun Gong has today adopted an increasingly greater political stance against China's ruling Communist. Its New-York based information center puts out regular bulletins on its website and practitioners living outside of China hold demonstrations to publicize allegations that the Chinese government imprisons and "re-educates" tens of thousands of practitioners, and tortures and harvests the organs of countless others.

Many Falun Gong members continue to tout the movement's spiritual and health benefits and, in China, practice in secret. Others have left the movement due to political and social pressure or disillusionment over Master Li's grandiose assertions that he is an extraterrestrial being who can prevent the destruction of humankind. In an interview with Time Magazine in 1999, for example, Li claimed that aliens have corrupted mankind by inventing computers, airplanes and other machinery and they plan to replace humans through cloning. He knew this, he claimed, because he, alone, understood things that modern scientist couldn't explain.

HUMAN RIGHTS

The U.S. Bill of Rights guarantees American citizens freedom of speech, religion, press, petition and assembly – rights that Americans consider fundamental in a modern society. In China, though, an individual's rights to education, employment, health, welfare benefits and even leisure are valued above those for personal expression which, it is reasoned, could ultimately harm the community by causing unrest.[100]

Many of these social rights are delineated in China's constitution. Among them: **Article 42,** which gives citizens the right, as well as assigning them the "duty," to work; **Article 46,** declares that citizens of the PRC have the right and duty to receive an education; **Article 45** states that the old, ill and disabled will be provided with material assistance from the state; and **Article 43** gives working people the right to rest.

These entitlements were well guarded after the establishment of the People's Republic of China in 1949. Almost all PRC citizens were employed by the state. All schoolchildren received an education, and medical care was widely available and essentially free to all citizens. But as China moved towards capitalism, the goal of economic success began to take precedence over universal rights to jobs, education and social welfare.

Labor
Under **Mao Zedong**, all Chinese workers were guaranteed an income as long as they were able to work – a system that became known as the "**iron rice bowl**." But this lifelong security came at a price – the lack of freedom to choose ones place of employment, to start a private business, or to relocate without permission.

After China reformed in the 1980s under Deng Xiaoping, citizens gained the right to choose their jobs, to become entrepreneurs and to move to a new city if they wished. Millions of rural workers took advantage of these freedoms by setting up "family household" farms, starting small businesses or seeking work in other cities. **Migrant workers** who moved to urban areas were employed by the millions to do factory or construction work (especially in preparation for the 2008 Summer Olympics) or got jobs in the service industry. Others became sidewalk vendors.

The opportunity to work away from one's hometown increased rural incomes multifold. But migrant workers seeking to supplement family incomes also had to give up social benefits (e.g. retirement benefits, health

---

[100] The subordination of individual rights for the benefit of the community has its roots in Daoism, which promotes harmony in nature and the community, Confucianism, which advocates maintaining social harmony by observing and adhering to a hierarchy of relationships, as well as Buddhism and Mohism, which discourage the pursuit of frivolous pleasures.

care and low cost education) and were always at risk of losing their jobs. In 2008, more than 20 million people became unemployed when factories closed due to the shrinking demand for Chinese products overseas. Workers in Shanghai, Beijing and other large cities were eligible to receive Minimum Living allowances of about $35 a month from the government. But many laid-off workers in less wealthy regions received little or nothing from financially-strapped local governments.[101]

With such high competition for work in urban areas and because there is little oversight by the government, factory owners have been much less concerned about providing healthy working conditions than their Western counterparts. Employees are often housed in overcrowded dormitories and frequently work 16 hours a day, six or seven days a week, to earn about $50 a month.[102] And although the legal working age is 16, many under-aged children have been sent to work in factories, especially for those tasks requiring small hands and sharp eyes, by families who could not afford school fees [103] and needed the extra income.

Mine workers, in high demand because of China's increasing demand for coal, endure the most appalling working conditions. Hundreds of thousands of coal miners have suffered from pneumoconiosis, a lung disease caused by the inhalation of harmful dust, and thousands have died each year in mine accidents.

Health care
Before economic reforms, health care, although not of the highest quality, was widely available to all citizens. To serve the most outlying areas, the Communist government trained "**barefoot doctors**" to provide first aid to remote villagers. Those rural doctors helped increase China's life-expectancy from 35 years of age in 1949 to 65 years just thirty years later.

Today, many Chinese citizens in the countryside cannot afford medical care. Because of cuts in subsidies by cash-strapped local governments, hospitals are forced to supplement their operating expenses by charging high prices for medications and diagnostic tests and charging fees for medical treatments. The reluctance of people in the countryside to seek medical care has been particularly detrimental during outbreaks of contagious diseases like

---

[101] Each year, hundreds of thousands of unemployed workers demonstrate to demand unpaid benefits, pensions and unpaid back wages. The unrest is one of China's biggest threats to social stability.

[102] Chinese workers are not permitted to join unions which could protect them from employees who withhold payment or exploit workers in other ways, for example, by confiscating their official papers to keep them from leaving or charging them outrageous prices for room and board.

[103] All Chinese schoolchildren are required to attend at least nine years of school but the quality of teachers and facilities in the countryside lags far behind those in the cities leaving children unprepared to pass national competitive exams to advance to the next level. Furthermore, although no tuition is charged, parents are required to absorb the costs for books and other fees which can put a great financial burden on poor families. Poor parents are also greatly pressured to pull kids out of school early to help with the family business.

SARS, the respiratory ailment that killed hundreds of people and infected thousands, Avian or "bird" flu, tuberculosis and *enterovirus*, a highly contagious and sometimes fatal hand, foot and mouth disease.

In 2009 the Chinese government announced plans to overhaul the health care system by building hundreds of thousands of village clinics, putting price caps on hundreds of prescription drugs, increasing subsidies and expanding medical insurance to cover 90% of the population by 2011.

Rights
As in the United States Constitution, China's Constitution also lists freedoms protected by the government.

- **Article 35** guarantees citizens of the PRC freedom of speech, of the press, of assembly, of association, of procession and demonstration.

- **Article 36** grants citizens the freedom of religion (see page 72) as long as practicing the religion doesn't disrupt society.

- **Article 37** states that no citizens may be arrested except with the approval of a people's procuratorate or by the decision of a people's court. And arrests must be made by a public security organ. Unlawful detention or deprivation of a citizen's freedoms by any other means is prohibited and unlawful search of citizens is prohibited.

- **Article 38** protects the dignity of citizens by prohibiting insults, libel, false accusation or false incrimination.

- **Article 39** protects citizens from inviolability of the home.

- **Article 40** states that no organization or individual may, on any ground, infringe on a citizen's freedom of privacy of correspondence "except in cases where to meet the needs of state security or of criminal investigation, public security or procuratorial organs are permitted to censor correspondence…"

- **Article 41** gives citizens of the PRC the right to "criticize and make suggestions regarding any state organ or functionary" as long as the facts are not distorted. The state organ concerned, in return, must deal with complaints made by citizens in a responsible manner and no one may "suppress such complaints" or "retaliate against the citizens making them."

Unlike in the United States, however, China's application of these rights has been inconsistent.

"Freedom to Assemble," "Freedom to Demonstrate"
In 1978, Chinese activists took advantage of the Central Government's temporary tolerance for dissent by posting poems and articles on a brick wall in Beijing dubbed the **Democracy Wall**. The posters criticized the Gang of Four and the shortcomings and excesses of China's previous regimes. The exercise

took place during a period called the "**Beijing Spring**," when Chinese citizens were permitted to publicly air their grievances.

The brief experiment with freedom of speech ended a year later when disgruntled Chinese began directly criticizing the party and demanding fundamental changes. Most objectionable to Deng Xiaoping was activist Wei Jingsheng's essay calling for the institution of a "**fifth modernization**" – democracy – to be added to the government's goals of modernizing agriculture, industry, technology and defense. After the posting, Wei was imprisoned until 1993 for "passing military secrets."[104]

Ten years later, the April 1989 death of pro-reformist former Secretary General **Hu Yaobang** sparked a large-scale demonstration that convinced the government to put an end to political reform.

The protest would become known in the West as the **Tiananmen Square Massacre** and the **June 4th Incident** to the Chinese (to distinguish it from the Tiananmen Square demonstration that brought down the Gang of Four in 1976). It began as a mass mourning ceremony for the politician who advocated political reform and who had rehabilitated many officials who had been unjustly purged by the Maoists. Within days, though, hundreds of thousands of students joined the gathering turning the event into a rally for freedom and democratic reform and a protest against corruption. To restore order, the government enacted martial law. When that didn't work, **Deng Xiaoping** and his conservative supporters (who feared a return to the political chaos of the Gang of Four period) deployed tanks and ordered soldiers to shoot at demonstrators. By June 4th, between 240 (the official Chinese figure) and 7,000 (according to NATO figures) civilians and soldiers had been killed in the melee.

The Tiananmen Square protest deeply troubled the Chinese Communist Party which immediately put a stop to democratic political reforms. Party cadres who showed any support for the students, such as General Secretary **Zhao Ziyang**, [105] were expelled from power or jailed and key protesters were arrested. Chinese media coverage of the event was banned (although foreign journalists, who had been in town to cover Soviet leader Mikhail Gorbachev's visit to China, sent reports about the protest and subsequent carnage, triggering an international outcry).

The Chinese Democracy Movement continued in secret in China and abroad, but demonstrations from that point on focused primarily on economic issues and local corruption.

---

[104] Wei was released in 1993 as a show of conciliation when the Chinese were hoping to win their bid to host the Summer Olympics. He was jailed again when they lost their bid and released again in 1997 for "medical reasons."

[105] Zhao Ziyang was replaced by Shanghai Mayor Jiang Zemin – who had earned the Party's trust by taking swift and decisive action against demonstrators in Shanghai.

Mass Incidents

Official estimates report that more than 100,000 "mass incidents" (riots, demonstrations and street protests) occur every year throughout China. Most of these involve rural Chinese citizens who have become frustrated by the widening economic gap between poor country folks and the wealthy urban population.[106] Other uprisings have involved Chinese workers who have lost their jobs, migrant workers who have been forced to return home, families that have lost their homes because of deals made between developers and crooked local officials, mine workers demanding better pay and safer working conditions and civilians angered over negligent or corrupt police activity. The growing frequency of these events, especially after the 2008 economic crisis, not only mocks the dream of a "harmonious society" but has become a threat to national security and the Communist Party. (see the National Human Rights Action Plan 2009-2010 pg. 87)

Privacy of Correspondence

Article 40 of China's Constitution guarantees citizens of the PRC the "freedom of privacy of correspondence," "except in cases of public security or criminal investigation." But this liberty doesn't extend to internet e-mail, chatrooms or blogs. Chinese citizens who send messages over the internet containing incendiary terms such as "Falun Gong," "Dalai Lama," "Democracy" or "Tiananmen Square" risk being apprehended by China's "cyberpolice" and disciplined.

Under the guise of protecting the populace from pornography, terrorism and other threats, the Chinese government has set up a sophisticated system of "packet sniffers" that scan web traffic for hundreds of potentially subversive terms and pictures – with the controversial collaboration of international companies like Yahoo! and Google.[107]

Sample of Blocked Internet Terms
Falun Dafa
Li Hongzhi
Tiananmen massacre
SARS
Zhao Ziyang (and zzy)
Central Propaganda Department
Cat abuse
Foot and mouth disease
Hire a killer
Chen Shui-bian (Taiwan's president)
East Turkestan (Xinjiang)
Chinese Politics
China liberal
Pollution lawsuit

Users who search for banned websites are met with blank screens or "site not found" messages.[108] Those who use objectionable terms or leave subversive comments on online forums receive transmitted warnings to behave. Repeat offenders risk being reported to the police by the owners of China's many

---

[106] It is estimated that 90% of China's richest people are related to senior officials.

[107] All web traffic in China is routed through just three centers in Beijing, Shanghai and Guangzhou. Yahoo and Google, among other service providers, have been under fire for self-censoring their search engines and turning over suspect emails to Chinese authorities.

[108] Tech-savvy users are usually able to get around the "Great firewall of China" by redirecting inquiries through other sites.

"Jingjing" is one of two cartoon internet police characters displayed on web pages in Shenzhen to remind users to self-regulate their online behavior.

"cybercafés" who, by law, must keep detailed records of customers' web usage.[109] Reporters Without Borders estimates that about 50 cyber-dissidents are currently serving time in prison, although the number could be larger.

Freedom of the Press

China's guarantee of "freedom of the press" is quickly and regularly violated by the Communist Party's Propaganda Department (CDP) or its administrative agencies, the General Administration of Press and Publications (GAPP)[110] and the State Administration of Radio, Film and Television (SARFT)[111] if they deem that a story "endangers the country" in any way.

Journalists generally avoid reporting on China's relations with Taiwan, the June 4th Incident, air pollution, Tibet or other taboo subjects. To be safe, independent media outlets also rely on stories filtered through China's official news service **Xinhua**, which owns dozens of newspapers and magazines printed in six language.

Journalists who do not abide by the rules can be dismissed, demoted or even imprisoned – as was the fate of at least thirty Chinese journalists accused recently of "providing state secrets," "plotting to subvert the government," or otherwise "endangering state security."[112] Hundreds of news outlets have also been closed or fined for printing "internal" information, publishing "false reports:[113] or violating the 2007 "Emergency Response Law" – a law banning the spread of "unverified information" on riots, industrial accidents, natural disasters, health and public security crises and other emergencies.[114]

---

109 Chinese citizens who wish to surf the web have to register with the local police department and must provide I.D. cards before using public computers. No one under age sixteen is allowed in a cybercafé.

110 The GAPP formulates guidelines and policies for the news publishing industry and monitors news publishing activities. It is also responsible for investigating and prosecuting illegal publications and illegal activity in print and on the Internet.

111 The State Administration of Radio, Film and TV (SARFT) drafts policies pertaining to radio and TV propaganda and creates film and video guidelines. Television and radio shows must be endorsed by SARFT before being broadcast.

112 Journalists, bloggers and others deemed dangerous by China's propaganda machine have also been forcibly admitted to psychiatric hospitals (e.g. activist He Weihua), or sent to labor camps.

113 One newspaper was criticized for reporting that Sun Yat-sen was a Korean. Another for writing a negative report on a Pharmaceutical Group and another for writing a "false report" about a Chinese navy ship's escort mission to Somalia which "harmed the reputation of the Chinese Army."

114 The "Emergency Response Law" was written in reaction to media reports during the 2003 SARS outbreak. The law has had the effect of muzzling the press preventing from reporting on incidents like mine explosions for fear of being charged with inaccurate reporting.

Amnesty International has reported that China has the largest recorded number of imprisoned journalists and cyber-dissidents in the world. And according to Reporters Without Borders China ranks 162nd out of 167 countries on its global press freedom index – above only Eritrea, Turkmenistan, Burma, Cuba and North Korea.

Civil Rights

China has come a long way from the days of random arrests and persecutions under Mao Zedong. In 1979, the country established a law of criminal procedures and a criminal law code (both amended in 1996 and 1997[115] respectively); and **Article 125** of China's Constitution gives accused citizens the right to defense and a public trial. But the PRC continues to be widely criticized for violating its own rules.

Local authorities continue to illegally detain people or send criminals to "re-education labor camps" before they stand trial. And despite laws that outlaw beating and torturing detainees, there have been many reports of this kind of intimidation and violence by local police. Detainees are also susceptible to the political whims of Communist Party legal committees who may determine the outcome of a case before it goes to trial and often manipulate the proceedings.

> **State Security Law of the PRC**
> **Adopted Feb. 1993**
> **Article 4**
>
> "Any organization and individual whose conduct harms the PRC's state security must be dealt with by legal means. Acts of harming the PRC's state security [include]:"
> 1. ... plotting to subvert the government, dismember the state and overthrow the socialist system
> 2. ...taking part in an espionage organization or accepting a mission assigned by an espionage organization or its agents
> 3. ...stealing, secretly gathering, buying and illegally providing state secrets for an enemy
> 4. ...instigating, luring and bribing state personnel to rise in rebellion
> 5. ...engaging in other sabotage activities against state security.

Currently China has about 140,000 lawyers, one for every 9,000 people (the U.S. has one lawyer for every 300 people). Chinese lawyers have represented miners and farmers against state-owned companies, citizens whose properties have been appropriated through eminent domain, parents whose babies were sickened by melamine-tainted milk, Falun Gong members, Tibetans and other plaintiffs and defendants – but not without risk. According to Amnesty International, at least four lawyers have been threatened with violence by authorities for defending clients in high-profile and controversial cases in the first four months of 2009 alone. Many more were prevented from meeting with clients or had their licenses revoked.

---

[115] The revised criminal law included more than 250 additions among them: laws against money laundering; insider trading; copyright infringement; internet crimes (spreading viruses); producing and selling food or medicines of dangerously inferior quality and other crimes. It also dropped the category of "counterrevolutionary crimes" and replaced it with a section on endangering state security.

In some cases where the crime is weakly defined, charges for greater, more abstractly defined crimes have been applied; for example charging a cyber-dissident or journalist with "transmitting state secrets," (see box on pg. 86) which, by law, may deprive the defendant of the right to employ a lawyer for defense. Other tactics taken to compromise citizens' legal rights include preventing the accused from notifying families or lawyers in time to build a defense, and harassing or detaining litigants – as was the case when families sought legal action against corrupt officials for building shoddy schools that collapsed during the 2008 Sichuan earthquake.

"Inviolability of the home"
Chinese law dictates that PRC citizens must be fairly compensated for property appropriated by the state for public use. With China's rapid development, this law is frequently invoked by families who have complained of inadequate compensation for homes that have been demolished to make way for the many construction projects in China's cities and in the countryside.

In recent years, entire neighborhoods have been razed in developing cities to make room for shopping malls, high rises, office towers or highways. Former residents must make do with what the government deems is fair compensation (which often is far below the actual value of the property) and relocate to less affluent parts of town.

> **Three Gorges Dam Displacement**
>
> More than a million people living in a thousand villages near the Yangtze River were relocated to prepare for rising waters resulting from the construction of the **Three Gorges Dam**, a $25 billion hydroelectric project expected to provide China with more than 18,000 megawatts of electricity by 2009. In 2007, it was announced that an additional four million people would be encouraged to move from their homes near the dam to the Chongqing metropolitan area by 2020. When the dam is completed, 13 cities, 140 towns and more than 1300 villages will be submerged.

In the countryside, farmers do not own the land they cultivate but rather "lease" it from the state or the village collectives. This arrangement leaves them with little protection from corrupt village officials who can earn big kickbacks from selling the land to developers for a hundred times its value as farmland. Land seizures of this type have left tens of millions of farmers jobless and homeless. Without a way to seek legal redress, farmers have had no choice but to resort to staging sometimes violent protests to convey their frustration. And many have landed in jail for "inciting to subvert state power."

National Human Rights Action Plan of China (2009-2010)
In response to calls from the United Nations and human rights groups in the West for China to improve its human rights record and to appease citizen's growing dissatisfaction with local security forces, the Chinese leadership issued a human rights action plan in 2009. The timing of its release, before two significant anniversaries, the 50th anniversary of the failed uprising in

Tibet against Chinese rule and the 20th anniversary of the Tiananmen Square protests, was intended to avert potential demonstrations.

The document reemphasized human rights protections outlined in China's constitution and the country's criminal laws. It also established timelines determining when action would be taken to improve living conditions.

As promised in the plan, the government would be increasing its efforts to promote employment, raise incomes, build more affordable housing and solve the nation's food problems. The government would also increase old-age pensions and expand national basic health services by constructing thousands of hospitals and improving the quality of available medical care. Infectious diseases (including AIDS) would be brought under control, 120 million more people would have access to safe drinking water[116] by 2010 and community sports facilities would be built to accommodate national fitness programs.

Education: By law, all children in China must attend school for at least nine years. According to the goal stated in the plan, the state would take measures to ensure that 99% of China's children would be enrolled in elementary schools and 98% would enter Junior High schools – including the children of migrant workers. In rural areas, where educational standards lag far behind those in the city, the state pledged to pay teachers their full salaries on time and renovate school buildings. As an incentive, teachers who volunteered to teach in western China would receive free tuition for their Master's Degree in Education.

Farmers: According to the plan, laws regarding land rights would be redefined and farmers' rights to own and use their land would be protected. Anyone violating the regulations on land management would be punished. The plan also called for a more equitable distribution of basic public services.

Sichuan Earthquake: To appease people living in the Sichuan province hit by the May 12, 2008 earthquake, the government planned to make sure that every family would have a house to live in as well as an income from employment and social security. Schools and hospitals would be rebuilt in affected areas and the names of people who were killed or disappeared would be made public.

Civil Rights: The document reemphasized the state's prohibition of illegal or prolonged detention by law enforcement personnel. It also reiterated the prohibition of insult, abuse and torture to extract confessions and ordered that police stations keep a physical separation between detainees and interrogators and conduct physical examinations of detainees before and after an interrogation. In cases where that right is violated, the state would compensate victims and punish those responsible for the illegal activity. For a detainee's convenience, the state would provide letter boxes for complaints in detainee's cells.

---

[116] Water in China contains contaminants such as fluorine, arsenic or schistosomes.

Fair Trial: Along with guaranteeing the rights of litigants to a lawful, timely and impartial trial, all trials would be videotaped. The plan also guaranteed lawyers the right to meet with clients in custody and conduct investigations and the state would work to extend convenient and sound legal aid to the poor.

Right to be informed: The Chinese government would keep the public informed about government affairs by distributing government news releases to the press, promoting "E-government" and other measures.

Right to participate: Revisions would be made to the Election Law to improve the election system and efforts would be made to more fully incorporate ethnic minorities, women, farmers, migrant workers and other underrepresented groups in the People's Congress. Efforts would also be made to enhance the level of villagers' self-governance and to promote direct elections of urban neighborhood committee members. The government would solicit opinions from mass organizations (trade unions, women's federations etc.) when formulating laws, regulations and public policies. The government would open channels for people to make complaints by offering special telephone lines, online access and agencies to enable people to petition the government by letter, fax, email or other written forms.[117] Party and government leaders were urged to read letters from petitioners, make comments or issue orders, and receive visitors on a regular basis.

Ethnic minorities: In compliance with the stated aim to combat Han chauvinism, China's constitution prohibits any kind of discrimination against or oppression of any nationality. Along with securing the rights of minority nationalities, including protecting their freedom to use their own languages and preserve their customs, the state is committed to accelerating the economic and cultural development in areas inhabited by minority nationalities. The National Human Rights Action Plan of 2009 expands the state's responsibility by increasing funding to publications in minority languages, making sure that all 55 minority ethnic groups have representatives in the National People's Congress and the Standing Committee, enhancing local education and improving access to roads, electricity, telephone service, TV programs, clinics and safe drinking water. It also promotes the implementation of the **Law on Regional Ethnic Autonomy** which guarantees the rights of ethnic minorities to manage their own affairs.

---

117 Article 41 in the Constitution allows citizens to make official complaints against "functionaries." But the millions of Chinese petitioners with grievances often had to travel many miles to meet with high-level officials and risked detention, imprisonment or even violence in retaliation. Zhang Yimou's film "The Story of Qiu Ju" followed a rural wife's long journey up the bureaucratic ladder all the way to Beijing to file a complaint against the actions of a local village official.

ONE-CHILD LAW

In mid-2009, China's population was above 1.3 billion people – 2.6 times the number of people who lived in China in 1949 and one and a half times the population between 1969 and 1972 when China's birthrate was at its peak (the average of more than 6 births per woman). To Mao Zedong, more people meant more bodies to contribute to the country's defense and development. But in the opinion of Zhou Enlai, who was the first to attempt to limit the birth rate, uncontrolled population growth would eventually lead to a crisis.

Under Zhou Enlai's guidance in the 1970s, couples were encouraged to limit their families to two children born a few years apart. Slogans like "later, longer, fewer" (later marriage, siblings born at least four years apart and fewer children) and "one is good, two is okay and three is too many" were widely circulated. But despite the government's efforts, China's population reached a billion people by 1980 and was still growing, leading to concerns about how the government was going to provide education, health care and jobs to its people.

In order to forestall a disaster and foster the country's economic progress, Deng Xiaoping and his supporters went beyond propaganda to making it compulsory. Under a law enacted in 1979, couples would only be permitted to have one child or face legal and financial consequences – with some exceptions.

Families who had more than one child would be charged large fines, would have to pay for education and health care for all of their children (which could amount to more than a quarter of a family's budget) and could be denied bonuses at work or even lose their jobs, among other penalties.

Exceptions were made if both parents were only children, if one or both parents were ethnic minorities or, in the countryside, if the first child was female or disabled.

Fertility rates dropped dramatically from 3.3 births per woman in 1970 to about 1.5 at the end of the decade. It is estimated that the one-child law is responsible for about 400 million fewer people in the world today.

However, the law has had consequences. The one-child provision, although universally unpopular, has been largely accepted in the crowded cities, where parents tend to work outside the home and childcare and education are expensive. In the countryside, though, the law is widely resisted.

Traditionally sons in Chinese culture are cherished because they carry on the family name and are expected to take care of their parents in their old age and after their death by visiting their graves to honor their memory. Females, by contrast, customarily join their husbands' families and bring a marriage dowry with them. Daughters, therefore, are considered less valuable in rural households. And with the one-child law, some parents have taken desperate measures to ensure that that child is a son.

Since the law has been enforced, the number of abandoned girls has risen dramatically. Before the practice was outlawed in China, some pregnant women also resorted to taking ultrasound tests to identify the gender of their child and then aborting female fetuses. A few cases of female infanticide have also been reported.

Through the years these practices have created a skewed male to female ratio in the country with men outnumbering women by tens of millions.[118]

The one-child policy has also had other unintended consequences. Only children are doted on by two parents and four grandparents creating a generation of "little emperors" who have no siblings or cousins to compete with. Once these kids get older, though, they are responsible for taking care of their parents and grandparents.

Loopholes in the policy have also highlighted the income gap between rich and poor. Wealthy city dwellers who wish to surmount the legal restrictions can afford to pay the fines for having more children or find other loopholes, for example hiring surrogates to carry babies, giving birth to children in foreign countries or relying on fertility drugs and embryo implants to produce twins or triplets, for example.

---

[118] The imbalance of males to females also means that a great number of men are left without wives, a discrepancy that has produced an underground matchmaking industry that sometimes involves abducting baby girls.

TIBET

Surrounded by the highest mountains in the world, Tibet is cut off from the rest of civilization. For many years its borders were closed to foreigners giving it an aura of mystery that was popularized in James Hilton's 1933 novel <u>Lost Horizon</u> as the land of the mythical city of Shangri-La ("La" is Tibetan for mountain pass).

Called the "Roof of the World," this arid plateau with an average altitude of 14,700 feet[119] has become one of the most contentious regions in the world. Known as the **Tibetan** or **Xizang Autonomous Region (TAR)** to the Chinese and simply "Tibet" or "**Bod**" to its inhabitants, the region and the fate of its exiled spokesperson, the **Dalai Lama**, (called "His Holiness" by his followers) has inspired activists from across the globe including actors Richard Gere, Sharon Stone, Steven Seagal, Paris Hilton and others who support Tibet's freedom.

Tibetans, Western supporters and Human Rights organizations claim that the PRC has been persecuting the local population and destroying Tibetan Buddhist culture. They call on China to release Tibet from China's hold by granting the country independence.

The Chinese Central Government claims that Tibet has been part of China for centuries and feels it has done much to modernize the region and improve local living conditions.

TIBET'S HISTORY

According to legend, the early **Bon**-practicing[120] Tibetans were first ruled by King **Nyatri Tsanpo**, a mystical king who descended from the sky on a magical rope ladder. At the end of his time on earth, the king climbed back up the same ladder back up to heaven. His successors came and left the earth the same way until the ladder connecting earth and the heavens was cut around 100 B.C. condemning the 8th king to a human death.

In the 7th century A.D., Tibet (or "**Bod**") was united and expanded by **Dharmaraja** ("King of Truth") **Songtsan Gampo** (r. 627-649). As the boundaries extended throughout Central Asia and along the Silk Route, Tibetans came into close contact with Buddhists from India to China. The connection was strengthened when Songtsan married two Buddhist princesses – one from China (**Wencheng**, the niece of powerful Emperor **Taizong** of Tang China, see pg. 10) and another from Nepal – and instituted a code of law based on Buddhist principles.

---

[119] At 12,000 feet in elevation, Tibet's capital, Lhasa, is the world's highest capital. Mt. Everest, which lies on the border between Tibet and Nepal is the highest mountain in the world rising above 29,000 feet.

[120] The Bon religion combined animistic and shamanistic beliefs. Animism is the belief that spirits or souls exist in animals, plants, mountains and lakes. Practitioners of Shamanism believe they can communicate with the spirit world through priests or shamans.

The Tibetan Empire reached its zenith in the 8th century under **Trisong Detsen** (r. 755-97) – even occupying the Chinese capital of Chang-an (present-day Xi'an) in 763 while China was in the midst of the chaos of the **An Shi Rebellion** (see pg. 11).

During his reign, King Trisong declared Indian Buddhism the official religion, invited Indian Buddhist scholars to his court, supervised the translation of scriptures and sponsored the construction of Tibet's first Buddhist Monastery (**Samye**) in 775. (Buddhism in Tibet is also called "**Lamaism**" after its priests or "lamas.")

But the growing popularity of Buddhism under Trisong and his successors threatened to diminish the status of Tibetan nobles and **Bon** priests who rose up in revolt. After **King Tri Ralpachen**, a supporter of Buddhism, was killed in 836, **Langdarma**, his brother who succeeded him, ordered the destruction of Buddhist temples and persecuted monks and nuns. The internal strife (worsened by pressure from Kyrgyz refugees and other external troubles) fractured the Tibetan Empire into a number of small princedoms plunging Tibet into a four-century-long bleak period. The disunity left Tibet too weak to resist the forces of **Genghis Khan's Mongol** hordes when they swept through the region in the 13th century.

The Mongols had already conquered northern China, central Asia and Russia before turning their attention towards Tibet which they conquered in 1230. Impressed with Tibetan Buddhism (which had survived the 9th century persecution), the Mongols under the rule of Genghis Khan's grandson, Mongolian prince **Godan Khan** eventually adopted the religion. Godan Khan, who converted to Buddhism in 1247, had been influenced by **Kunga Gyaltsen**, (the **Sakya Pandita** [Wise Scholar]), a revered Tibetan Buddhist *lama* from the **Sakya** school who had been invited to the Mongolian court to be a spiritual guide. In 1249, the Mongols appointed Sakya Pandita as Viceroy of Tibet giving him temporal authority over western Tibet.

> **MAIN SCHOOLS OF TIBETAN BUDDHISM**
>
> • Nyingma
> • Sakya
> • Kagya
> • Gelug

The Sakya Pandita's nephew and successor, **Drogon Chogyal Phagpa** (1235-1280), also impressed Godan Khan's successor, **Kublai Khan,** who appointed him his spiritual guru. After founding the Yuan Dynasty in 1271, Kublai Khan gave Phagpa and the Sakya priests great authority over the whole of Tibet. For the duration of the "priest-patron" relationship established under Kublai Khan, Tibet enjoyed a higher degree of autonomy than other areas of China during the Yuan Dynasty. But the privilege ended a few years after Kublai Khan's death in 1295.

The dominance of the Sakya priests weakened in the early 14th century. In their place arose the **Kagyu Order** (Black Hat Sect) whose priests were welcomed because they shared the Tibetans' popular desire to free themselves from the influence of outside rulers.

Despite the efforts of the Ming emperors (who had overthrown the Mongols and established the Chinese Ming Dynasty in 1368) they were unable to establish the same patron-priest relationship enjoyed between the Mongols and Tibetans. By most accounts, Tibetan leaders paid tribute to Ming leaders but remained largely independent.

Gelug Order (Yellow Hat Sect)

At the time of the Ming Dynasty in China, spiritual master **Tsong Khapa** (or Tsongkapa 1357-1419) founded the new **Gelug Order** of Tibetan Buddhism which allowed ordinary people to progress on the path towards enlightenment. The Order spread widely throughout Tibet after Tsong Khapa's death in 1419.

The Gelug (or **Gelugpa**) Order was headed by a spiritual leader or **Ganden Tripa** (who was appointed based on the results of a competitive examination) and a temporal leader, the **Dalai Lama** (literally "Oceanic Master"), believed to be the incarnation (embodiment) of the **Bodhisattva**[121] **of Compassion.**

A monk from the Gelug Order, **Sonam Gyatso**, was the first to receive the title of **Third Dalai Lama** in 1578. He was believed to have been the reincarnation[122] of the **Second Dalai Lama, Gendun Gyatso** (1476-1541) who was, himself, the reincarnation of **Gendun Drup** (1391-1474). The title of Dalai Lama was bestowed on both of them after their deaths.

The designation of the **Fourth Dalai Lama** (1589-1617), the great-grandson of Mongolian leader **Altan Khan,** was rejected by supporters of the **Kagyu Order** who tried to take his power away. He died in 1617 under suspicious circumstances at age 35.

His reincarnation, the **Fifth Dalai Lama, Ngawang Lozang Gyatso**, was the first to wield significant power over Tibet. After defeating a rebellion by the rival Kagyu priests, the Fifth Dalai Lama assumed both spiritual and political power over Tibet, proclaimed Lhasa the capital of Tibet, and transformed the government. In 1653, the Great Fifth Dalai Lama was invited to Beijing by the Manchu Qing Emperor, **Shunzhi** (see pg. 19) and, some say, honored as an equal. While other world leaders were moving towards secular modernity (Louis XIV in France, Peter the Great of Russia, the Tokugawa Shoguns in Japan for example), the Fifth Dalai Lama was modernizing Tibet spiritually including building the magnificent **Potala Palace,**

---

[121] A Boddhisatva is a being who is bound for enlightenment (*nirvana*) but chooses to remain on earth in order to help others attain it.

[122] When the Dalai Lama dies a search is made throughout Tibet for his successor/reincarnation - a child is selected and must demonstrate his authenticity by being able to correctly identify possessions held by the previous Dalai Lama and through other signs.

a 13-story, 1000-room monastery and temple that served as the seat of government.

In order to complete construction of the Potala Palace and to prevent hostile neighbors from taking advantage of the country's instability, the death of the Fifth Dalai Lama in 1682 was kept secret until his reincarnation (the Sixth Dalai Lama) was located and enthroned 15 years later. But the **Sixth Dalai Lama (Tsangyang Gyatso)** turned out to be a disappointment to the Gelug community. Tsangyang Gyatso preferred to drink wine, enjoy the company of women and write love songs rather than attend to affairs of the state. His rebelliousness damaged the relationship between Tibet and the Manchu Qing Emperors and provoked an invasion by the **Dzungar Mongols** who kidnapped the Sixth Dalai Lama and attempted to install an imposter after he died in captivity. When the Dzungars began to loot the holy places of Lhasa in 1717, the Manchu Qing Emperor **Kangxi** stepped in (see pg. 19).

By 1720, the Qing forces had expelled the Dzungars from Tibet and annihilated the Dzungar population. A year later, the Qing Emperor Kangxi, hailed as a liberator by the Tibetans, appointed the **Seventh Dalai Lama** and declared Tibet a protectorate of China.

PANCHEN LAMA

In 1642 the Fifth Dalai Lama honored his teacher by conferring upon him the title of **Panchen Lama** (meaning great [a contraction of Tibetan word *chenpo*] scholar [from Sanskrit word *pandita*]). The Panchen Lama is the second highest rank of lama after the Dalai Lama in the Gelugpa sect of Tibetan Buddhism.

The identity of the 11th reincarnation of the Panchen Lama is a matter of great controversy. After the 10th Panchen Lama died in 1989, the Chinese government created a committee to find his reincarnation from among 28 young boys born around the time of the 10th Panchen Lama's death. From the candidates, the Dalai Lama approved of one boy, **Gedhun Choekyi Nyima**, deeming him the Panchen Lama's true reincarnation. The Beijing Committee, however, named 6-year old **Gyaincain Norbu (Qoigyijabu)** the 11th Panchen Lama and put the boy chosen by the Dalai Lama and his family into "protective custody."

In his teens, Beijing's choice for Panchen Lama, **Qoigyijabu**, began publicly expressing support for the PRC's central government and accused the Dalai Lama and his "separatist clique" of planning to ruin Tibet's social stability and ignoring Tibet's successful development under Chinese rule. Qoigyijabu is greatly valued as a propaganda tool within the PRC despite the fact that his status as Panchen Lama is rejected by most Tibetan Buddhists.

In 1725, the Qing government installed Chinese commissioners or **Ambans** to oversee temporal affairs of the country. The Chinese military intervened again in 1788 and 1791 to defend Tibet against an invasion by **Gurkhas** from Nepal. After the second intervention, the Qing strengthened the authority of the Ambans giving them control of Tibet's foreign affairs and defense.

The Qing also instituted a system to determine future incarnations of the Dalai Lama by pulling names of young candidates from a **golden urn**. The **10th, 11th** and **12th Dalai Lamas** were selected this way before the Qing government began to weaken and the system was abandoned.

Unlike the previous three Dalai Lamas who were seen as mere figureheads manipulated by Manchu emperors, the Thirteenth Dalai Lama became a symbol of Tibetan authority.

The **Thirteenth Dalai Lama (Thubten Gyatso)** born in 1876, grew up while China was preoccupied with internal rebellions and battles with European colonialists and he assumed political power in the midst of the **"Great Game"** – a geopolitical competition between **Britain** and **Russia** for dominance over Central Asia.

In 1904 the British began to fear that Tibet, dangerously situated on the northeast border of Great Britain's precious Indian colony, was becoming too friendly with Russia. To prevent an alliance from forming and to compel Tibet to sign a trade agreement, the British sent an expedition led by **Sir Francis Younghusband**. The British were particularly intrigued by stories of gilded Buddhas and other treasures and were eager to discover the source of the gold.

Younghusband marched towards Lhasa trying to avoid bloodshed by negotiating with the Tibetans but at Gyantse (Gyangze) they met up with a troop of "poorly armed" Tibetan soldiers. A shot was fired and a battle ensued leaving more than 1,000 Tibetans dead.

The Thirteenth Dalai Lama fled to Mongolia leaving a regent, **Ganden Tri Rinpoche**, behind to rule in his absence. To prevent further bloodshed the regent signed a treaty promising not to enter into any relations with a foreign power without British approval while giving the British free trade rights.

Although Britain had acknowledged China's suzerainty over Tibet in a number of treaties (among them the 1876 **Chefoo Convention** giving the British the "right" to send an expedition to Tibet), the Qing Emperor feared British expansionism. In order to reassert their authority, the Manchus deployed Chinese troops and occupied important Tibetan centers. The Dalai Lama, back from Mongolia, was once again forced to leave Tibet in 1910, this time seeking refuge in British India. But the Emperor's hold on Tibet quickly weakened just a year later when news of the **1911 Xinhai Revolution** and the fall of the Qing Dynasty reached Lhasa.

The Chinese troops mutinied and then, in 1912, were expelled from Tibet. The 13th Dalai Lama returned the same year and assumed spiritual and temporal rule over a peaceful and independent Tibet until his death in 1933. Tibet's freedom had lasted almost four decades before the Chinese Communists defeated

Chiang Kai-Shek's Kuomintang army in 1949 and turned their sites westward.

Soon after Mao Zedong declared the establishment of the People's Republic of China, the Communists were determined to "liberate" Tibet from feudal rule and reintegrate the lost region back into China. The threat of the impending attack

prompted the Tibetans to quickly endow 15-year old **Tenzin Gyatso**, the **Fourteenth Dalai Lama**, with full powers on November 1950, years earlier than planned. The next year, Chinese troops marched into Lhasa forcing the Tibetans to sign a **17-Point Agreement** that affirmed China's sovereignty over Tibet.

During the next several decades, the Chinese destroyed thousands of temples and monasteries and redistributed temple lands to the people. Religious practice (deemed Tibet's "poison" by Chairman Mao) was made illegal.[123] Priests and other Tibetans were arrested and imprisoned. And misguided agricultural reforms were enacted that destroyed crops and led to mass starvation. More than a million Tibetans were reported to have died as a result of Chinese policies.

The Tibetans tried to resist by staging a mass uprising on March 10, 1959 but the rebellion was violently put down by Chinese troops – thousands of people were killed and many more, especially monks and nuns, were jailed or deported.

Fearing that his own death would seal Tibet's fate, a few days after the **Tibetan National Uprising** the Fourteenth Dalai Lama fled to India with 80,000 followers. The refugees set up a government-in-exile in Dharamsala, India where the Dalai Lama would continue to fight for Tibetan

freedom as spiritual and temporal head of the Tibetan Central Government.

By 1962 eastern Tibet had been completely annexed by China and three years later, western Tibet became the **Tibetan Autonomous Region.** In the mid-1960s, Tibet, along with the rest of the PRC, fell victim to the **Great Proletariat Cultural Revolution** (see pg. 40) aimed at ridding China of anything symbolizing the **Four Olds**: "Old Customs, Old Culture, Old Habits and Old Ideas." Fanatic Chinese Red Guards who had made their way to Tibet zealously destroyed many remaining monasteries and terrorized the population before the Cultural Revolution came to an end in the 1970s.

---

[123] Religion is such an important part of Tibetans' lives that one boy from every family is obliged to join the monastery. Many Tibetans make pilgrimages to the Jokhan Temple in Lhasa, the most important and sacred temple in Tibet, some walking for hundreds of miles prostrating themselves at each step. Flags with prayers like "Om Mani Padme Hum" (the Buddhist mantra that roughly means "Om 'jewel in the lotus' hum) written on them adorn monasteries and houses and are even strung out across the highest mountain passes so that the wind can carry the prayers all over the world.

Conditions in Tibet improved in the 1980s when the central powers official-ly denounced Han Chinese chauvinism and celebrated the ethnic diversity of China's 56 recognized "nationalities." The 1982 Constitution guaranteed minorities the right to use their own languages and "to preserve or reform their own folkways and customs." Ethnic groups were represented in the National People's Congress and, in 1984, the government enacted the **Regional Ethnic Autonomy Law (REAL)** granting autonomous govern-ments the authority to formulate regulations reflecting the local minority culture – as long as they didn't directly contravene central policy.

By law, Tibetans in the Tibetan Autonomous Region (TAR) enjoy self-government rights. The **Tibetan New Year** (Losar) and **Shoton** (literally the "Yogurt Banquet"[124] also called the Tibetan Opera Festival) are recognized as public holidays, and all laws and government documents are to be written in both Chinese and the Tibetan language. Tourists were allowed to visit Tibet in the early 1980s and by 1987 the Tibetan flag was permitted to be flown. Two years later, the Dalai Lama was awarded the Nobel Peace Prize

TERMS
• **Tibet Autonomous Region (TAR)** The area of U-Tsang and western Kham. The TAR is governed by Tibetans and overseen by a general secretary from the Chinese Communist Party (in the 1980s Hu Jintao served as General Secretary of Tibet)
• **Historic Tibet** Area that once included the Tibet Autonomous Region and eastern Kham and Amdo. Today Historic Tibet is distributed among the provinces of Qinghai, Gansu, Sichuan and Yunnan.
• **Central Administration** The Tibetan government-in-exile headed by the Dalai Lama

for his commitment to non-violence. But despite the fact that his Holiness had dropped his demand for outright Tibetan independence (asking instead for more autonomy for the Tibetan people), the Chinese government refused to let him return to Lhasa.

According to the constitution, the Chinese Central government is devoted to upholding the cultural development of minority nationalities in autonomous areas. But it has also taken on the responsibility of assisting the area eco-nomically. Millions of dollars have been poured into Tibet's development in the last decade and, in order to boost its economic power and better assimi-late the region into the PRC, Han Chinese have been offered great financial incentives to relocate to Tibet and open up businesses.

Viewed as progress to the Chinese and a cultural tragedy to Tibetans and Western sympathizers, Chinese-sponsored development has slowly

---

[124] Traditionally, monks would reserve the month of June on the Tibetan calendar for medita-tion and self-awareness. At the end of the month, local Tibetans would offer them yogurt. In the 17th century, operas were added as a part of the festivities.

eroded Tibetan culture while the hundreds of thousands of immigrant Chinese have displaced local businesses. In some towns like the capital and spiritual center, Lhasa, Han Chinese outnumber Tibetans and discotheques, bars and other Sino-centric businesses have been established causing deep resentment.

On March 14, 2008, the 49th anniversary of the failed 1959 coup, local resentment came to a head in one of the largest demonstrations seen in Tibet in decades. Grievances by monks and nuns protesting the detention of monks combined with those of the general population angered over Han Chinese favoritism, unemployment, education and housing issues and governmental policies sparked a deadly four-day riot in Lhasa and regions of China with high concentrations of Tibetans.

The Chinese claimed the riot had been orchestrated by the Dalai Lama at a time when all eyes were on China in the days approaching the 2008 Summer Olympics. The Dalai Lama said the uprising was spontaneously motivated by widespread discontent with the Chinese government.

Beijing also said that 22 people, predominantly Han Chinese, died during the rioting and blamed Tibetans rioters for great damage to Chinese-owned businesses. The Tibetan government-in-exile said that Chinese troops killed 220 Tibetans, injured almost 1,300 and arrested more than 5,000 people in the course of the protests.

In February the following year, Tibetans commemorated the 2008 uprising by refusing to celebrate the Tibetan New Year, normally the most festive holiday of the year. The Chinese declared a week-long holiday celebration with fireworks and pageants but the Tibetan families defiantly prayed in the temples or at home.

In order to prevent a repeat of what the Chinese call the **3-14 Riots** in March

2009, the Chinese government stationed police on the streets of Lhasa and banned all foreigners until April 2009. Pro-Chinese officials also dubbed March 28 "Serf Emancipation Day" to celebrate the day they say they liberated Tibetans from a brutal feudal regime.

CHINESE PERSPECTIVE

The Chinese state that, except for the period between 1911 and 1950, Tibet was always a part of China. They accuse the Dalai Lama and his Western backers (the CIA among them) of trying to tear China apart by calling for Tibetan Independence. Mao Zedong and the Communists also believed that they were "liberating" Tibet from feudal and theocratic oppression. Today the Chinese pride themselves for modernizing Tibet by infusing billions of dollars into the region to build schools, hospitals and infrastructure and introducing a healthier Chinese diet.[125] They believe the Tibetans should be grateful for the aid.

TIBETAN PERSPECTIVE

The Tibetans claim 1300 years of independence from China beginning with the first unification of the country under Songtsan Gampo in the 7th century, continuing with the "priest-patron" relationship the Tibetans had established with the Mongols in the Yuan Dynasty and including administrative independence under the Manchus of the Qing Dynasty. The Tibetans consider the current occupation a cultural genocide. Western sympathizers believe the Chinese should give Tibetan full independence although His Holiness, the 14th Dalai Lama has said he would agree to an autonomous status similar to that enjoyed by Hong Kong under the "one country, two systems" arrangement.

---

[125] The Tibetans' staple food consisted primarily of roasted barley flour (*tsampa*) and yak-butter tea. (Butter made from the milk of the female yak is widely used to make tea and molded into butter sculptures [*forma*] as offerings). The Chinese introduced meat, rice and vegetables adding nutrition to the Tibetan diet.

TAIWAN
(Republic of China)

The status of Taiwan has been an issue since the **Kuomintang** led by **Chiang Kai-Shek** made the island its home base in 1949. (see pg. 36) The **PRC** (People's Republic of China) considers Taiwan a renegade province of China. The government of the **ROC (Republic of China)** claims Taiwan is not a part of the People's Republic of China. Rather than battle it out, both governments have adopted a policy of deliberate ambiguity which allows the two entities to peacefully engage in trade.

BACKGROUND:

When the Europeans were exploring the Asian seas in the 16th century, Taiwan was already populated by Austronesian aborigines. The indigenous tribes periodically attacked merchants who landed on the shores of **"Ilha Formosa"** or **"Beautiful Island,"** as the Portuguese called it, but they could not prevent the eventual settlement of Taiwan by colonizers from Portugal, Spain and Holland in the 17th century.

In 1662, the Dutch were expelled by **Koxinga,**[126] a Chinese military leader and opponent of the ruling Qing dynasty, who turned the island into a base for anti-Qing activities. Koxinga's heirs held the island for twenty years after Koxinga's death but they were defeated in 1682 by the Qing Emperor **Kangxi** who annexed Taiwan and made it a part of southern China's Fujian Province. For the next two hundred years, Fujian residents crossed the strait from mainland China to Taiwan to escape famine and war.

Taiwan was lost to the Japanese after the first **Sino-Japanese War** of 1895. According to the terms of the **Treaty of Shimonoseki** ending the war, Taiwan was to be ceded to the Japanese "in perpetuity." The island became Japan's supplier of rice and sugar and, during **World War II**, served as a staging area for Japan's invasion of Southeast Asia.

Upon Japan's defeat at the end of World War II in 1945, the **UN Relief and Rehabilitation Administration** placed Taiwan under the administrative control of the **Nationalist Kuomintang (KMT)** who were rec-

---

126 Koxinga is considered a hero to Chinese on both sides of the Taiwan Strait. Mainland Chinese adulate him because he brought Chinese sovereignty back to the island. Taiwanese see him as a heroic rebel against Qing rule.

101

ognized as the leaders of the Republic of China.

The end of World War II also brought an end to the temporary truce between the Chinese Communists led by **Mao Zedong** and the KMT under **Chiang Kai-shek**. A year after the Japanese had been defeated, China was engaged in a full-blown civil war.

Despite hundreds of millions of dollars in aid and weapons from the United States, the KMT could not defeat Mao's Communist forces. In April 1949, the Communists captured **Nanjing**, the capital of the KMT's Republic of China, and the **Nationalists** were surrounded in the countryside and towns across China. When Mao Zedong proclaimed the People's Republic of China on October 1, 1949, Chiang Kai-shek and more than a million surviving KMT forces retreated to the island of Taiwan where they continued their fight to reclaim the mainland.

In March 1950, Generalissimo Chiang Kai-shek formally resumed his role as President of the **Republic of China (ROC)** in **Taipei**, Taiwan and declared martial law. The KMT estimated that with America's help, it would take three years for the communist government to collapse allowing the KMT to reclaim the mainland. Until then, Taiwan would be in a state of war and the government would operate in emergency mode.

Meanwhile, the United States became engaged in a proxy war when North Korea crossed the 38th parallel border into South Korea, a U.S. ally, in June 1950 (see pg. 37). Mindful of the PRC's support of the North Koreans, the U.S. positioned its Seventh Fleet between Taiwan and mainland China and provided the ROC with military and economic aid. The official position of the U.S. was not to help the KMT go to war against Communist China but to prevent the island from falling under the control of Mao's Communist government. Eventually Taiwan was incorporated into the U.S. defense system in the western Pacific.

Because of U.S. support, the ROC remained the internationally recognized government of China represented by a seat in the United Nations.[127] Improvements were made in education, construction and trade and the population became more worldly than its Communist counterparts across the strait. But Taiwan's privileged status took a turn in the 1970s.

On October 25, 1971, the General Assembly of the United Nations voted to withdraw the ROC's seat and recognize the PRC as China's sole legitimate government.[128] In February 1972, U.S. President **Richard Nixon** made his

---

[127] The Republic of China was one of the founding members of the United Nations in 1945.

[128] Since the passing of Resolution 2758 by the UN General Assembly, the ROC has since reapplied to become a member or even a participant in the UN and its affiliate organizations such as the World Health Organization. Its application has been denied by the People's Republic of China which has veto power.

historic visit to the PRC and, hoping to employ mainland China as a counterbalance to the Soviet Union, normalized relations between the two countries[129] (see pg. 42). Four years later, Chiang Kai-shek died, weakening the drive to reunify China under the KMT.

Although some people on the island continued to battle for ROC sovereignty over mainland China, most Taiwanese understood that the probability for success would be remote. Others turned their attention towards complete independence from the PRC which still considers Taiwan China's **23rd province** and its president a "provincial governor."

In order to avoid confrontation, both the PRC and the ROC and foreign nations dealing with both governments have adopted a policy of "deliberate ambiguity."

POLITICS

After 50 years of harsh foreign rule by the Japanese, the Taiwanese natives (or **"Formosans"** as they were then called) confronted what they saw as politically corrupt newcomers. On February 28, 1947, about 2,000 "Formosans" gathered in Taipei to protest against the beating of a local female cigarette peddler and the killing of a bystander by Chinese police agents. Under orders from Chiang Kai-shek, the ROC-appointed governor-general deployed military troops resulting in the deaths of thousands of Taiwanese civilians. The uprising was followed by a "white terror" of mysterious disappearances, imprisonment and executions.

Two years after the **228 Incident** (as the event was dubbed after the month [2] and day [28] of the rebellion), Chiang Kai-shek and the KMT fled mainland China to **Formosa** (Taiwan) where the Generalissimo enacted martial law and ruled with an iron fist. Because of the "emergency" **"Temporary Provisions Effective During the Period of Communist Rebellion,"** rival parties to the Kuomintang were outlawed and, despite term limits outlined in the ROC Constitution, President Chiang Kai-shek, and members of the the Legislature would be allowed to hold on to their posts indefinitely.

The KMT also attempted to "sinicize" the island by making Mandarin the national language, teaching children Chinese rather than Taiwanese history and generally suppressing the Taiwanese identity.

Chiang Ching-kuo (1978-1988)
Taiwan became slightly more open under Chiang Kai-shek's son and successor, **Chiang Ching-kuo** who served as ROC President from 1978 until 1988. The government still kept a tight reign on the political system, but Chiang Ching-kuo began to allow political dissent and relaxed government

---

[129] In 1972, the U.S. and PRC established the Shanghai Communiqué stating that neither of them would seek hegemony in the Asia-Pacific region. The U.S. also acknowledged that there existed only one China (One-China policy) and agreed to reduce its military support of Taiwan.

controls over speech and the press. Although still formally illegal, rival parties, for example the **Democratic Progressive Party** formed in 1986, were allowed to meet and Taiwan natives (such as **Lee Teng-hui**, Chiang Ching-kuo's successor) were slowly incorporated into the government. A year before his death in 1988, Chiang Ching-kuo also lifted martial law, ending the longest period of uninterrupted martial law in history, and permitted Taiwan residents to visit their relatives on the Chinese mainland.

Lee Teng-hui (1988-2000)
Lee Teng-hui, Chiang Ching-kuo's vice president, unlike the original members of the KMT, was born in Taiwan to a **Hakka**[130] family. He succeeded Chiang Ching-kuo as President of the ROC in January 1988 and became the first democratically elected Taiwanese president in 1996. Following the lead of his predecessor, Lee made major advancements in democratic reform ushering in an era of freedom and openness.

As the first Taiwanese (not "Chinese") president, Lee was a strong proponent of "Taiwanization," that is, the recognition of local culture, language and art over that of the Han Chinese. Because he spoke the local language (Hakka, a southern Fujianese dialect), he was trusted by the natives. And by promoting Taiwanese history, values, beliefs and culture he endeared himself to locals. But his presidency was also wrought with controversy.

In 1995, Lee caused a commotion when he attended an alumni retreat at his alma mater, New York's Cornell University, becoming the first Taiwanese leader to visit the United States. The Chinese were furious over the visit because it implied Taiwan's independence. In retaliation, the Chinese conducting missile tests in the Taiwan Strait. But rather than intimidating Taiwan, the missile tests only strengthened Lee's chances of winning the 1996 presidential elections.

Three years after winning a second term, Lee, emboldened, said he expected relations between Taiwan and the mainland to be conducted on a state-to-state basis provoking the PRC to suspend talks with the ROC.

Chen Shui-bian (2000-2008)
Chen Shui-bian, a member of the Democratic Progressive Party which advocated Taiwan's independence from China, won the 2000 presidential race on a promise to end political corruption.

Although his party promoted Taiwan's separation from mainland China, Chen pledged not to declare Taiwanese independence, change the name of the

---

[130] The Hakka (or "guest people") are a subgroup of the Han Chinese who settled in the Fujian, Jiangxi, Guangdong region of China in the 13th century. Many Hakka migrated to Taiwan during the Qing dynasty especially during and after the Taiping Rebellion (1850-1864). They currently make up about 15% of Taiwan's population.

"Republic of China" to the "Republic of Taiwan," push for the inclusion of the "state-to-state" concept of PRC-ROC relations in Taiwan's Constitution nor promote a referendum on the question of independence. He also promised he would not abolish the **National Unification Council**, an agency that had been formed in 1990 to promote Taiwan's unification with the PRC. Chen would uphold these **"Four Noes and One Without"** (as the declaration was known) as long as the PRC did not use force against Taiwan.[131]

However, under Chen Shui Bian, new passports were printed with the word "Taiwan" on the covers, the word "China" was replaced with the word "Taiwan" on postage stamps and it was proposed that Taiwan use years from the Gregorian calendar (dated from the birth of Christ as in 2007, 2008, 2009 etc.) on banknotes, IDs, drivers licenses, diplomas and other official documents instead of the year dated from the ROCs founding in 1912 (2009 would be the 98th year for example). There was also an attempt to change Taiwan's constitution.

All of these moves were interpreted by members of the pro-unification **Pan-Blue Coalition** (see box pg. 107) as attempts to move Taiwan closer toward independence and an affront to groups in Taiwan who had an affinity for China and Chinese culture.

Chen's second term was fraught with scandal. His wife was accused of money laundering and forgery, his son-in-law was charged with insider trading and Chen was accused of bribery and embezzlement.[132] The controversy and Chen's low approval rating at the end of his second term (down to 21%) helped the KMT candidate, **Ma Ying-jeou**, defeat the DPP party in the 2008 presidential race.

In order to avoid confrontation with the PRC (which objects to the use of the term "Republic of China" since it considers that government defunct or "Taiwan" because it implies that it is a separate country, the Taiwanese fly the "Chinese Taipei" flag during international sporting events such as the Olympics.

Ma Ying-jeou (2008 -)
During his campaign, Ma Ying-jeou promised that he would expand economic ties with Beijing and would not press for either independence or reunification with the mainland. In his first year in office, he launched direct charter flights between Taiwan and mainland China (before the changes, travelers had to fly through Hong Kong), opened Taiwan to mainland tourists and eased legislation allowing Taiwanese to invest in mainland Chinese businesses and vice versa.

[131] Adherence to the "Four Noes, One Without" policy was important to guarantee good relations with the United States which was allied with the PRC.

[132] Chen was arrested six months after he left office. His wife, his son and his daughter-in-law pleaded guilty to embezzlement and money-laundering and his son-in-law was imprisoned. Chen insisted that he was an innocent victim of a politically-motivated plot to discredit him.

ECONOMIC MIRACLE

In the 1940s, Taiwan's economy had been devastated by war. Railroads and harbors were not operating properly, prices were high and there were shortages of basic goods. The situation improved when the U.S., considering the island too valuable to fall into communist hands, aided Taiwan economically during the Korean war and the Cold War.

Free from the strict control of the PRC's authoritarian government, Taiwan was able to develop a market economic and liberal trade policies. Within Taiwan, the population, sharing the common and persistent threat of attack by Chinese Communists, embraced Confucian principles of self-sacrifice and striving as a group. Frugal living and hard work were also encouraged making Taiwan a competitive destination for nations looking for cheap but productive labor.

Between the 1960 and 1980, like fellow "Asian Tigers" of Hong Kong, South Korea, and Singapore, Taiwan's economy grew an average of 6-10% per year. Its success was based on the island's export-driven economic model, motivated and skilled workforce, high savings rate, low domestic consumption, high import tariffs and undervalued currency (all resulting in a trade surplus with industrialized countries).

Taiwan Today

The Republic of China is only recognized by 24 nations including Gambia, Belize, Paraguay, Nicaragua, the Dominican Republic and the Holy See of Vatican City. Although the United States supported the ROC after its creation in 1912, since America's allegiance shifted from Taipei to Beijing in 1979 the U.S. has tread a fine line between defending Taiwan against a communist takeover and preventing Taiwan from declaring independence. For example the U.S. chastised former ROC President Chen Shui-bian when his policies moved too aggressively toward separation from the mainland.

THREE COMMUNIQUÉS

Shanghai Communiqué (1972)
The Shanghai communique summarizes the agreement between the U.S. under President Nixon and the PRC represented by Premier Zhou Enlai. According to the Communiqué, the U.S. affirms that the Government of the PRC is the sole legal government of China and that Taiwan is a province of China. The U.S. further acknowledges that Taiwan's status is China's internal affair in which no other country has the right to interfere and agrees to withdraw U.S. forces and military installations from Taiwan.

Second Communiqué (1979)
The Second Communiqué reaffirm's that the U.S. recognizes the Government of the PRC as the sole legal Government of China. Within this context, the U.S. will maintain cultural, commercial and other unofficial relations with the people of Taiwan.

Third Communiqué (1982)
The Third Communiqué reemphasizes the two earlier treaties and reiterates that the U.S. Government has no intention of infringing on Chinese sovereignty and territorial integrity or interfering in China's internal affairs by pursuing a policy of "two Chinas."

America's policies towards Taiwan are dictated by the **Three Communiqués** with China (which outlined the terms of the normalization of relations between the U.S. and the PRC) and the 1979 **Taiwan Relations Act** which authorized the continuation of commercial and cultural relations between the U.S. and Taiwan.

TERMS REFERRING TO TAIWAN

- **Republic of China** (ROC) – The Republic of China was established in January 1, 1912 by Dr. Sun Yat-sen to replace the Qing monarchy.
- **Kuomintang or Nationalist Party** – The KMT is the oldest political party of the Republic of China (ROC). The KMT was defeated by the Chinese Communists led by Mao Zedong in 1949 forcing its members to flee to the island of Taiwan where the government of the Republic of China was reestablished.
- **Chiang Kai-Shek** – Chiang Kai-shek became the leader of the Kuomintang after Sun Yat-sen's death on March 12, 1925 serving until his own death in 1975.
- **One-China policy** – The principle that China as a whole is made up of mainland China, Hong Kong, Macau and Taiwan. Both the Republic of China and the PRC hold this principle to be true – although there is disagreement over the nature of the sole legitimate government.
- **Democratic Progressive Party (DPP)** – The DPP was founded in September 1986 as an opposition party to the KMT. The first DPP candidate to win the presidency was Chen Shui-ban in 2000.
- **Pan-Green Coalition** – Created by three political parties including the DPP and Lee Teng-hui's Taiwan Solidarity Union in 2000, the Pan-Green Coalition promotes Taiwan independence over reunification with China.
- **Pan-Blue Coalition** – In opposition to the Pan-Green parties, the Pan-Blue coalition (which includes the KMT as a member and is named after the KMT party's official color), favors greater economic ties with the PRC and a Chinese nationalists identity.
- **Taike** – A slang term (and former insult) describing a distinct style adopted by Taiwanese youths who have shunned Western, Japanese and Chinese trends for uniquely lower-classed Taiwanese styles. Taikes can be seen wearing cheap flip-flop sandals, chewing betel-nuts, rolling up Mild-Seven cigarette boxes in the sleeves of T-shirts, dyeing their hair or dancing to techno music wearing white gloves among other activities.
- **Ethnic groups (CIA Factbook)** – Taiwanese (including Hakka) 84%, mainland Chinese 14%, indigenous 2%
- **Taiwan Relations Act (TRA)** – Adopted in January 1979, the Taiwan Relations Act authorizes the United States to continue close and friendly commercial, cultural and other relations between the people of the U.S. and the people on Taiwan in order to maintain peace, security and stability in the Western Pacific. The TRA also allows the U.S. to provide Taiwan with arms of a defensive nature and establishes the American Institute of Taiwan to perform consular services and cultivate cultural exchanges.

OTHER BOOKS BY AMANDA RORABACK

IRAQ in a Nutshell

IRAN in a Nutshell

AFGHANISTAN in a Nutshell

ISLAM in a Nutshell

PAKISTAN in a Nutshell

ISRAEL-PALESTINE in a Nutshell

To order books and for more information about Enisen Publishing,
the Nutshell Notes series and author Amanda Roraback
please visit www.enisen.com or e-mail publishing@enisen.com.

For more information about China and other countries,
please visit www.worldinanutshell.com.